The Associated Press Guide to News Writing

FOURTH EDITION

Rene J. Cappon

About Peterson's

Peterson's® has been your trusted educational publisher for more than 50 years. It's a milestone we're quite proud of, as we continue to offer the most accurate, dependable, high-quality educational content in the field, providing you with everything you need to succeed. No matter where you are on your academic or professional path, you can rely on Peterson's for its books, online information, expert test-prep tools, the most up-to-date education exploration data, and the highest quality career success resources—everything you need to achieve your education goals. For our complete line of products, visit **www.petersons.com**.

For more information, contact Peterson's, 4380 S. Syracuse St., Suite 200, Denver, CO 80237; 800-338-3282 Ext. 54229; or visit us online at **www.petersons.com.**

Peterson's makes every reasonable effort to obtain from reliable sources accurate, complete, and timely information about the tests covered in this book. Nevertheless, changes can be made in the tests or the administration of the tests at any time, and Peterson's makes no representation or warranty, either expressed or implied, as to the accuracy, timeliness, or completeness of the information contained in this book.

ISBN: 978-0-7689-4373-3

Printed in the United States of America

10 9 8 7 6 5 4 3   25 24 23

Fourth Edition

Contents

NEWS WRITING FOR THE DIGITAL AGE—AN INTRODUCTION

Foreword

This book is aimed at a select audience: Those who care about precise and attractive use of the language.

If you are in that company, read on. For here you will find—in a mix of humor, common sense and only occasional editorial pique—a guide to help you achieve what should be every journalist's aim, telling the reader what you mean in a crisp and correct way.

Perhaps the problem is the speed with which daily journalists must do some of their work. Perhaps it is that sameness of some of what we write— today's baseball game being normally not very different from yesterday's, this week's council meeting straying into predictable clichés, today's news briefing advancing us little if at all toward better understanding of the subject.

Whatever the reason, the problems that persist in everyday news writing are not hard to identify, and it is to these that this manual speaks.

We talk here not of an idyllic newsroom where the final four-paragraph accounts of auto accidents can be the leisurely product of a third and fourth rewrite. No, we deal here with what the careful writer (and editor) can do in a busy newsroom to bring to news copy the clarity and the appeal it must have at a time when so many other activities beckon for the reader's attention.

So, good writing is a practical matter; the story must be written well if it is to be read well.

But more tellingly, it is a professional matter. We should feel pride in doing our jobs well and in fulfilling our obligation to serve the reader well.

In the tumult of the last decade, as journalists have found themselves caught in unaccustomed legal and professional controversy, thousands of speeches have been given in defense of what we call "the people's right to know."

Let us also recognize the people's right to understand and be entertained. In support of this right comes this guide to the careful use of our most precious asset—the word.

LOUIS D. BOCCARDI

President and Chief Executive Officer, The Associated Press (1985–2003)

Preface

"From a writer's point of view, the best circumstance is to have Jack Cappon, in the flesh as your editor. Next best is to have at hand, for consultation or merely occasional picknicking, a collection of his ideas on the use of language," wrote Jules Loh, a special correspondent for the Associated Press in the preface of the previous edition of this text. Indeed, though Cappon died in 2007 and so much about the news industry seems to have changed since these words were first published in 1982, his ideas about language and newswriting remain relevant today. The basic principle that writers must focus on technique while handling daily deadline pressures still matters in an era of constant publication, which the internet enables for both professional and citizen journalists.

René Jacques Cappon was born in Vienna in 1924. German was his first language, but one of five he eventually studied. Of those, English "seduced him," Loh wrote. After finishing high school in New York and attending the University of Iowa, Cappon worked at the Associated Press for more than a half-century. He started in bureaus in Baltimore, Frankfurt and Kansas City before becoming a legendary editor. He oversaw the New Features department from 1958–1962 and again from 1977–1989. In that role he oversaw multiple Pulitzer Prize winners on a desk known affectionately as the "Poet's Corner." In 1989, he moved into a new role teaching writing throughout the AP and to newspapers. Given the reach of the AP into every corner country, it is hard to think of a more consequential role.

The Associated Press is still the news lifeline of this country. It was the internet before there was an internet, long before the massive technological upheaval of the mid-1990s and beyond. Its iterative, get-to-the-point style of writing dominates in the digital era. The wire service was a live blog before anyone knew those words, sending stories as it learned of them, changing the approach as details emerged; these are still core news skills. Readers saw the finished product in their morning newspaper, unaware of the skill and effort necessary to produce each article.

Cappon's words are still vital to sense makers and storytellers today. There are more demands on a writer's time and attention than ever before and, as innovations in the way news is reported and delivered proliferate, the unrelenting speed of information makes clarity vital. We live economy of language daily as we try to squeeze out thoughts via Twitter or on social media, where saying what you mean in as few words as possible is essential. Frankly, Cappon's focus on developing good writing habits is a necessity because we inhabit a world with fewer editors like Jack Cappon.

What follows in this reissue preserves much of Cappon's original writing and wit. Everyone who commits words to the page for a living, on some level, shares what Loh described as a visceral romance with the language. This book updates some examples and adds context for the digital era. But the text reminds us that good writing has a timeless quality, even if it is used to produce something as ephemeral as a news story.

Author's Note

Any word book like this guide is, in a sense, a collaboration. My collaborators have been numerous; I count among them the people on the staffs of The Associated Press and AP member newspapers who have been subjected to writing workshops I have given over the years. Rather than a systematic journalism manual, the book is extended shoptalk—a continuation of the discussions, formal and informal, with news writers intent on improving themselves in their craft.

Much news writing is, of course, done under deadline pressure, and it isn't always possible to hone and polish. But, too often, time limitations are invoked as an excuse for the kind of carelessness that springs more from poor writing habits than any other cause. Writers who trouble themselves about technique can adjust to these rush hours without turning slipshod.

Certain questions kept recurring at the workshops: How do I enliven my style? What's true color? How do I avoid limp leads without teetering into hysterical ones? What makes for good feature writing?

Much of the AP guide is devoted to such practical matters. I have tried to show what works, what doesn't, and why, as much by examples from copy as by commentary. These snippets of instructive prose stem mostly from the AP report, which was naturally handiest for me, with others from newspapers around the country.

I owe a debt to these largely anonymous contributors, triumphant or limping in the heat of the daily battle.

I also owe specific debts. I am especially grateful to AP Special Correspondent Jules Loh, who edited *The Associated Press Guide to News Writing* with gentle wisdom. I owe thanks, too, to Executive Editor (now AP President) Lou Boccardi, who read the manuscript and offered valuable suggestions and criticism.

For errors that have slipped through this fine screening, I bear sole responsibility. I suppose that some will be found; a corollary to Murphy's Law states that anyone who writes a book on writing will inevitably commit some of the gaffes he warns against. Some readers no doubt will find certain judgments of mine open to question—as too dogmatic, too lenient or altogether wrongheaded. Perhaps so. What matters more to me is the hope that this work might stir some writers, new and old, to think more about the process of writing, to remember that the first duty of language is to communicate, and that words can be the best of friends or the worst of enemies.

R. J. C.
New York, 2000

Chapter 1

Language: Pompous, Pedantic and Plain

News writing should be clear, concise, accurate and interesting. No one dissents from that proposition. But news is perishable, deadlines glare, resources are finite, big stories break unannounced—the pulse of daily journalism keeps racing. How much quality writing can you expect under such conditions?

But granting a measure of endemic disorder in the news business, which includes an ever-growing list of responsibilities and distractions, it's also true that much excellent copy is being written daily. And a far more curious fact emerges from a study of news writing in many places: Stories written at relative ease show much the same flaws as those written under pressure.

This clearly suggests that something outside the deadline process is at work. Reporters know they should write simply and strip clutter from their prose. Yet at the keyboard, amnesia sets in.

"To write well is as difficult as being good," said Somerset Maugham. There may be a connection. To be good takes a high level of moral awareness. To write well takes a high level of technical awareness. We usually lapse from inattention, not ignorance. We fudge the small, measured steps, the care for details, that craftsmanship demands.

And so it happens that a portion of the news report is like a river in flood, sweeping along a great many things that shouldn't be there: trees, drowned raccoons, front porches, old shoes. The sight can be heartrending.

Start with such tiny clutter as the "up" in "free up" or "head up." Contemplate "ongoing" or "currently," as in "he is currently the president of ... ," where the verb already expresses the sense of the adjective.

1

Swollen sentences heave into view: "The administration is going ahead despite the fact that opposition in Congress is rising." That would have been "... despite rising congressional opposition," if the writer had stayed awake.

Even stranger: "Good military and business strategy dictate avoidance of any action that places one in a position where others can call the shots." In his better moments, the writer would say, "... dictate that you keep the upper hand." Ten words saved.

And nearly inscrutable: "Yet, he said, humans oddly realize their limited finitude, and by the very fact that they do, transcend it in awareness of some further being of potential infinity." These are the problems that, in our limited finitude, we create for ourselves. (Another is journalese, our own tribal dialect, which is the subject of a later chapter.) News writers are professionally exposed to language bloat, jargons pumped into the atmosphere by official news sources and "communicators" in the bureaucracy, the professions, institutions and corporations.

Reporters are obligated to translate gobbledygook into plain English. Yet often they get stuck in the viscous verbiage of their sources. Even in the reporting on schools, a subject close to so many readers, pedagogues' jargon oozes into print. Libraries are promoted to *resource centers*. Classrooms become *classroom situations*, and classes become *learning experiences*. Kids who won't study are *underachievers*. The teacher's effort to encourage them becomes *an attempt to raise motivational levels*. The principal who wants calm in the classroom *proposes viable new goals in behavior modification*. Little Marsha's shyness is *difficulty to relate to her peer group*. None of this does much for the writer, and it does much less for Ms. Jones, the reader who wants to know what's going on in her local school.

The fatal lure of wordiness, abstraction and jargon is hardly new. More than 40 years ago George Orwell, a master of the plain, forceful style, deplored the same tendencies.

Contemporary writing at its worst, he noted in his essay on *Politics and the English Language*, doesn't choose words for the sake of their meaning but consists of "gumming long strips of words together that have already been set in order by someone else." He translated a verse from Ecclesiastes to illustrate the prose this leads to:

> I returned and saw under the sun, that the race is not to the swift, nor the battle to the strong, neither yet bread to the wise, nor yet riches to men of understanding, nor yet favor to men of skill; but time and chance happeneth to them all.

In modern bureaucratese:

> Objective consideration of contemporary phenomena compels the conclusion that success or failure in competitive activities exhibits no tendency to be commensurate with innate capacity, but that a considerable element of the unpredictable must invariably be taken into account.

This is parody, but not greatly overdrawn. A CEO speaks of "restructuring corporate culture" and "anticipated synergistic impacts on future profitability and employment levels." He's a cackle away from a federal agency's branding of horses and hens: "grain-consuming animal units." A parachute drop on Grenada was a "predawn vertical insertion." A civilian type came up with "fourth-quarter equity retreat" for the '87 stock market crash. And what's death on the operating table but a "substantive negative outcome"?

No one has appointed journalists as the guardians of the language, which goes its own way anyhow. But self-preservation should prompt us to combat imbecilities in our own copy. Our treasury is words. We can't afford to convert them into nonperforming assets, in the bankers' delicate phrase. Our sources often use words in ways that obscure meaning. The journalist's job is to make those meanings plain to an interested reader.

We are free to avoid hand-me-down phrases, official cant, the staccato of journalese. Our words then will be measured to how things really happen, how they really look and feel.

Take the following example. AP staffer Larry Neumeister captured the complex emotions about the death of Osama bin Laden for family members of those who died on 9/11, mixing clear description with direct quotations.

> Nearly 10 years after his wife was killed at the World Trade Center, Charles Wolf still falls asleep each night on one side of his bed.
>
> On Monday, news of the death of the man who helped orchestrate that emptiness brought Wolf a muted joy. He declared himself glad it was finally over still aware that, for him, it never really can be.
>
> "This is a feeling of happiness, but not jump-up-and-down happiness," said Wolf, who lost his wife, Katherine, in the attacks. "The idea of closure is something that really, really—it doesn't exist, to tell you the truth."
>
> Family members of those lost on Sept. 11 reflected Monday on a decade of grief that cannot be erased by any worldly victory. Still, the death of the shadowy figure who had taken pleasure in their sorrow brought some a sense of relief.

"I'd like to think that all the people who were murdered on Sept. 11 are cele-brating," said Maureen Santora, whose firefighter son, Christopher, was killed in the collapsed towers. She said she knows her son, who died at age 23, would have been "dancing in the streets" at word of bin Laden's death.

"I can hear him up in heaven yelling and screaming," she said. "I can see him being just thrilled."

But she, too, said there would be no closure for her. Instead, "There will be a hole in my heart until the day I die," she said.

Finally comes the chilling start of a story from Rwanda by AP corre-spondent Mark Fritz. His coverage of the unspeakable massacres in that little African nation won him a Pulitzer Prize.

KARUBAMBA, Rwanda (AP)—Nobody lives here anymore.

Not the expectant mothers huddled outside the maternity clinic, not the fam-ilies squeezed into the church, not the man who lies rotting in a schoolroom beneath a chalkboard map of Africa.

Everybody here is dead. Karubamba is a vision from hell, a flesh-and-bone junkyard of human wreckage, an obscene slaughterhouse that has fallen silent save for the roaring buzz of flies the size of honeybees.

With silent shrieks of agony locked on decaying faces, hundreds of bodies line the streets and fill the tidy brick buildings of this village, most of them in the sprawling Roman Catholic complex of classrooms and clinics at Karubamba's stilled heart.

Karubamba is just one breathtaking example of the mayhem that has made beautiful little Rwanda the world's most ghastly killing ground.

Karubamba, 30 miles northeast of Kigali, the capital, died April 11, six days after Rwandan President Juvenal Habyarimana, a member of the Hutu tribe, was killed in a plane crash whose cause is still undetermined.

The paranoia and suspicion surrounding the crash set off decades of complex ethnic, social and political hatreds. It ignited a murderous spree by extrem-ists from the majority Hutus against rival Tutsis and those Hutus who had opposed the government.

All this is straightforward and effective. No clichés, no superlatives; just the sort of detail that will make readers see as well as understand.

Not every news subject can be handled in exactly that style, but all news writing should aim for similar simplicity and directness. That is the message of this book. The rest is amplification.

Chapter 2

News Writing: Information Is Not Enough

Someone once asked Ernest Hemingway why he had kept doggedly rewriting the final chapter of *A Farewell to Arms*—supposedly 44 times. The answer: "To get the words right."

It's always a struggle to get the words right, whether we're a Hemingway or a few fathoms below his level. What first springs to mind is seldom good enough. Writing is the art of the second thought.

The humble grunts of daily journalism work under constraints that novelists don't have to worry about, but some second thought there must be—even if only for a few minutes when time is short, as it often is.

To gather information is not enough at a time when Americans are flooded with it by other sources, be it the churn of social media or the 24-hour patter of cable news. We need to make the reports we provide not only reliable but compelling enough to withstand the hurricane of competition.

The daily print newspaper may be sputtering. But online media have brought readers and writers closer together. We no longer write for an imagined readership. We can see what they are clicking on in real time; we can both follow their lead and introduce them to unexpected topics. In the late print era, "reader friendly" became a catchphrase in the news business.

Today it is simply clear that we must write *to* readers, not at them, in language attuned to their lives and everyday experience—language plain but not dull, terse yet relaxed, standard English that's correct but neither stilted nor high-flown. There may be easier ways to make a living, but then, what's more satisfying than the craft, the art, of storytelling, which is what we do when at our best?

Clarity, precision, a sense for detail and other virtues needed to see us through rarely arrive unbidden. They must be coaxed and nurtured.

News writers should ask themselves three questions before letting go of a story:

1. Have I said what I meant to say? The writer of the following sentence didn't quite make it:

   Covenant House later conceded that it had provided the young man, Kevin White, with a new identity, using the birth certificate of a 10-year-old boy who died in 1980 without permission from the child's parents.

   What parents would grant that sort of permission?

2. Have I put it as concisely as possible? The writer of the following sentence, from a story about a California brushfire, may well have thought so:

   Twelve rescue ambulances stood by to rush injured persons to nearby hospitals.

   But on second thought, it becomes clear that eight of those 12 words are drones. Ambulances are rescue vehicles; they don't dawdle; they always carry the injured, not the hale and hearty; and they rarely search for the remoter hospitals. Four words are all you need: *Twelve ambulances stood by. And even that could be pared to Twelve ambulances waited.*

3. Have I put things as simply as possible?

   The relationship between Congress and bureaucrats is one of symbiosis.

   Sure, the word *symbiosis* fits nicely, and it's fine for some audiences. But how many ordinary readers would understand it? So why not say, "Congress and bureaucrats feed off each other" or "depend on each other"? The phrases give the sense in plain language.

   The company expects significant synergy from the merger.

   Synergy is a corporate buzzword (and seldom an actual result). Longer but less mysterious:

   The company expects that the joined businesses will be more productive than the sum of their parts.

Details, you might say. But attention to detail is at the heart of good writing. As a sports announcer might say, it's a game of inches. Get careless with clauses and a sentence becomes a black hole from which no light escapes. Misplace a modifier and a serious passage becomes a grinning farce. Let an indefinite pronoun float free of its moorings, and you create a mystery about who does what to whom.

There's no solace in the thought that many readers will be able to figure out a muddled sentence. They should not be asked to. They should not be required to guess, to pause, to backtrack or to slog through a swamp of superfluous words. They'll find better things to do.

WASTED WORDS, WASTED SPACE

Nowhere is the case for economy with words stated more persuasively than in *The Elements of Style* by William Strunk and E. B. White:

> Vigorous writing is concise. A sentence should contain no unnecessary words, a paragraph no unnecessary sentences, for the same reason that a drawing should contain no unnecessary lines and a machine no unnecessary parts. This requires not that a writer make all his sentences short, or that he avoid all detail and treat his subject only in outline, but that every word tell.

All news writers past their novitiate understand the need to save words, but many of us are voluble by nature.

It's a matter of habit, starting with the small, innocuous phrase: *in the event of* for *if, despite the fact that* for *in spite of, adverse weather conditions* for *bad weather, take into custody* for *arrest.*

Many sentences can be improved by surface trimming. In the following example, just omit the italicized words:

> WASHINGTON—The administration is writing *new* regulations *designed* to sweep away many years of *accumulated* red tape and let local governments decide *for themselves* how to spend major urban aid grants.

Often, slight rewording produces dramatic results. Compare the original sentence (left) with the revision on the right:

It is unusual in the Legislature to have a conference with more than four members.	A conference committee with more than four members is unusual.

The IRS said that a number of Oregon complaints had been received as of Friday. Investigators are now in the process of checking out the possible violations.	The IRS said a number of Oregon complaints had been received as of Friday. Investigators are checking them out.
Consumers were slower in repaying installment debt in August and quicker in adding new debt in August than earlier this year, the government reported.	Consumers were quicker to borrow and slower to repay debt in August than earlier this year, the government reported.

Five, eight and five words are saved, respectively. The shorter versions are crisper. Eliminating tedium and saving words go hand in hand:

Israel *is not in favor of* a Mideast peace conference.	... opposes ...
The Senate Ethics Committee can vote *for the expulsion of*	... to expel ...
The union will *conduct a poll of* its members.	... poll ...
The Iranians hope *for the re-equipment of* their armed forces.	... to re-equip ...

These small phrases conspire to obscure meaning. Here is a sampling of what writers said and what, in context, they meant:

announced the names of	identified
Detroit area residential and real estate holding	in the Detroit area
responds specifically to incidents	responds to incidents
for the entire distance of the flight	for the flight
use his persuasive powers on behalf of	support
not yet known	unknown
can produce liver degeneration	can damage the liver

so it can afford to re-equip its fleet with new fuel-efficient jets	so it can buy fuel-efficient jets
now is asking for the relaxation of	wants to relax

THE ANEMIA OF ABSTRACTIONS

Certain abstract nouns, perennials of newspaper usage, tend to create clusters of surplus words: *issue, case, situation, question, condition, facilities, activities, experience, field, factor, proposition, basis, character, nature, process, problem.* Often these nouns are tacked onto specific words: heavy traffic becomes a *heavy traffic problem* or *the congested traffic situation.*

Besides being stuffy, these nouns are vague. What is a facility, an issue or a problem? A facility can be an airport, a hotel, a park or a kitchen. An issue is anything people discuss or disagree about. A health problem can be an ingrown toenail or terminal cancer.

A man who gets his throat slit in a dark alley is *a victim of violence,* but much is lost in the transcription. That is how abstract words work. Call a spade a spade and you evoke a clear picture. Call it an agricultural implement and you might be talking about a plow, a rake or an air-conditioned tractor.

Obviously, these long-faced, abstract nouns have some use, but the following examples show why you should treat them with reserve:

The *situation* poses a danger to the public because of the tendency of persons on probation to commit more crimes.	It's risky because people on probation often commit crimes.
On the *issue* of welfare payments, the committee deferred action for three weeks.	The committee deferred action on welfare payments for three weeks.
The government decided to replace him with a general of more aggressive *character.*	The government replaced him with a more aggressive general.
Crimes of a violent *nature* are increasing.	Violent crimes are increasing.

The Legislature has threatened to suspend all strip mining *operations*.	... all strip mining.
Ample space for recreational *activities* was provided.	Ample recreational space was provided.
The bridge below Smithville has now become a practical *proposition*.	... has become feasible.
The loss of skilled workers will be a damaging *factor* in the economy of the industrial Midwest.	... will damage the economy of the industrial Midwest.
Another worrisome matter is the *question* of productivity.	Another worry is productivity.
They receive their checks on a monthly *basis*.	They receive monthly checks.
They agreed that their adventure in the woods had been a worthwhile *experience*.	... had been worthwhile.
Mathematics skills are considered a valuable learning *experience*.	They can learn much from mathematics.
He is an acknowledged leader in the medical *field*.	He is a leader in medicine.
Half of the town lives in *conditions* of abject poverty.	... lives in abject poverty.
The state's hospital *facilities* must be upgraded.	The state's hospitals must be upgraded.

PEOPLE POWER

Under the heading of "abstractitis," Fowler's *Dictionary of Modern English Usage* says: "Persons and what they do, things and what is close to them are put in the background and we can only peer at them as through a glass darkly."

Here are some examples:

Research has shown that accidents are proportionately more prevalent with motorcycle use and are of a more violent nature.

Nothing in that sentence acts on anything. There's no hint that it has anything to do with people. Put more concretely:

Motorcyclists *have more accidents proportionately than other* motorists and are more often killed or seriously injured, research has shown.

A state civil service examination to fill uniformed court officers' jobs "had grossly disproportionate impact on blacks and Hispanics as compared to whites," it was charged in a federal court suit today.	A state civil service examination to fill jobs for uniformed court officers was unfair to blacks and Hispanics, a federal court suit charged today.

The revision at right takes two words, *was unfair,* to say what the original version says in 13. Note also how the unpleasant noun pileup, *uniformed court officers' jobs,* is loosened up with a preposition.

Utilities were under a judicial mandate Wednesday not to cut off services during the winter months to elderly individuals and those whose lives would be put at risk due to their ill health.	A court ordered utilities not to cut off services to the elderly and seriously ill during the winter.

The revision specifies who is meant and where the order came from. Here are abstract blotches in an action story:

Police are "furious" over *a recent rash of objects* being thrown from highway overpasses at moving vehicles and say they are going to crack down on the *offenders* "before someone gets killed."

Police Detective John Smith said police have not been able to link recent wrecks involving serious injuries to the *overpass offenses* but added: "*We* just think that some recent accidents are related to this. It just seems too much of a coincidence."

As the story notes later, the little monsters were tossing bottles, rocks and bricks, which is livelier than *recent rash of objects.* Let details drive out generalities:

> Police say they are furious at youngsters tossing rocks and bottles from over-passes and intend to crack down "before some driver gets killed."

> Detective John Smith said police have been unable to link recent serious accidents to the rock throwers, "but it just seems like too much of a coincidence."

It's possible to be too specific, though, especially in crime and accident stories. Gory details don't necessarily add much except revulsion.

When a body long dead is recovered, it's superfluous to mention that it was *badly decomposed*. Nor was it useful to report, in a plane crash story, that *the flesh fell off some of the victims* who burned to death. *Charred beyond recognition* is another phrase you can usually dispense with. A man stabbed 20 times may be presumed to have bled; the writer need not dwell on the dimensions of a *pool of blood*. Limit the gore. For that matter, you often find a crime victim described as *fully clothed*, gratuitous when there is no reason to suspect otherwise.

You can't avoid abstractions entirely. Some stories must be carried on in abstract terms; try to lighten them with concrete illustrations. And abstract words save time and space on second and further references. That's fine, so long as they are preceded by particulars.

The following story, though, is the kind of disaster that happens when all defenses fail:

> LARAMIE, Wyo.—A University of Wyoming trustee committee has given its approval to drafts of reallocation criteria and processes despite concern over just who will be allowed to influence the process.

> The Academic Issues Committee approved the drafts during the first day of the trustees' two-day meeting.

> Some trustees want input from outside the university personnel rolls, but at least one member of the administration said he is concerned over the possible impact that might have.

> Trustee President Ford Bussart said he wants students and community members to have a say in the reallocation process because he thinks they will have valuable input.

> "There are items and matters which may not appear to have importance, which in fact, if viewed from other perspectives on the part of interested constituencies, indeed have importance," the Green River attorney said. "I simply fear that if we internalize the process completely and don't get those external points of view, we can find this process becomes nearly impossible to accomplish. Which can create problems for the university."

What's being reallocated? Who might influence the "process" and how? What are the "criteria"? Does "personnel rolls" mean the faculty, or anybody employed by the school? What are the "items and matters" referred to in the fifth graf? There's no way for the reader to dispel the fog.

Faced with such opaque language, we should at least try for a palliative—a concrete example.

That was done in a story about the introduction of a "theme-immersion" or "inquiry-based" method of teaching at a faltering school.

There, too, the educators spoke in nebulous generalities until questioning brought one administrator down to earth. Under "theme immersion," he said, teachers would introduce a single topic, for example, the weather:

> Students would learn everything, he said (or hoped), from the science of meteorology to the spelling of key words and the math skills involved in tracking a storm.

That's not much, but it does give readers something to hold on to. All professions use jargon, and knowing those magic phrases separates insiders from outsiders. Our job is to make that jargon intelligible to readers, not to repeat it.

Educators and academics are among the masters of linguistic befuddlement. When we fail to translate or at least exemplify, it becomes ours.

HOLD THE ADJECTIVES

Not every noun needs an adjective. Not every adjective needs an adverb. Not every writer has got the message.

E. B. White once observed that the adjective hasn't been born yet that can pull a noun out of a tight spot. Mark Twain, who also had writing experience, once told a young correspondent, "When you can catch an adjective, kill it."

He softened that a little: "*No,* I don't mean that utterly, but kill most of them—then the rest will be valuable. They weaken when they are close together, they give strength when wide apart. An adjective habit, or a wordy, flowery, diffuse habit, once fastened upon a person is as hard to get rid of as any other vice."

Some writers think killing adjectives is like clubbing baby seals; they can't bear the thought. But strong writing should rely on nouns and verbs. Pick the right ones and you'll need few modifiers. Use adjectives to make your meaning clear, not as decorative afterthoughts.

It is hard to see what the second adjective is doing in this sentence:

> The shots on the quiet Sunday morning sent passersby into *frightened* flight.

Quiet, yes. But *frightened* flight? As distinguished from courageous flight? Can we read the minds of the passersby? This second adjective has turned us into mind readers.

The lust for modification leads writers into other futilities. Certain nouns evoke inevitable adjectives that are only feebly descriptive. The combinations become clichés: *posh* resort, *sprawling* reservation, *hardy* natives, *devout* Catholic, *scenic* countryside, *colorful* scene, *high-powered* rifle, *picturesque* village and many more.

An onslaught of modifiers turns the following story into treacle:

> LONDON—The slim, almost boyish figure of the next king of England moved across the thick carpet of the elegant Brown's Hotel at Piccadilly. He signed the hotel register as cameras flashed.
>
> En route back to the enormous, black Rolls Royce outside, he suddenly stopped. He had spotted two young women working on a guest register in the lobby.
>
> "What are you doing?" he inquired politely in deep aristocratic tones. The receptionists looked up and their jaws fell.
>
> "The guest register, is it?" asked the immaculately groomed Prince Charles.

You would expect a prince to be polite and immaculately groomed and to visit an elegant hotel rather than a fleabag. Anyway, *thick carpet* suggests elegance. And what is *almost boyish*? What are *deep aristocratic tones*? Strike all modifiers except *thick, enormous, black* and *slim* and the intro recovers.

Keep your hands off nouns that need no additional voltage: *serious* danger, *stern* warning, *deadly* poison, *grave* crisis. The nouns do better without the modifiers.

A crisis is a serious turning point by definition. And the habit of mechanical modifying leads to many glaring redundancies, among them:

absolutely conclusive	exact counterpart
agricultural crops	future plan
awkward dilemma	general public
close proximity	grateful thanks
complete monopoly	hired mercenary
completely full	irreducible minimum
divisive quarrel	lifeless body
end result	lonely hermit
entirely absent	meaningless gibberish

mutual cooperation	personal opinion
new record	pragmatic realist
old adage	present incumbent
organic life	sworn affidavit
original founder	true facts
patently obvious	ultimate outcome
personal friend	

To test the logic of such modifiers, turn them around. Are there partial monopolies? Pleasant dilemmas? False facts? Impersonal friends?

Treat adverbial intensifiers with the same caution as adjectives. *Very urgent, highly unusual, extremely serious*—the adverbs add only shrillness. *Definitely* is generally expendable. *The ambassador will definitely leave tomorrow* says nothing more than that he'll leave. *Undue* can be particularly fatuous:

> State officials expressed the hope that people in the New Madrid area would show no *undue* alarm over the earthquake prediction.

What is due alarm? A good alternative would be ... *would remain calm.*

> Most of the victims of the heat wave were elderly and all succumbed after their body temperatures climbed to *extremely dangerous* levels.

Because all died, *extremely* is absurd and *dangerous* goes without saying. You might make it, ... *climbed to deadly levels.*

> The conservative group complained that the court was taking *undue* liberties with the Constitution.

Strike *undue.*

Adverbs like *relatively* and *comparatively* are usually mere padding:

> *Relatively* few senators answered the quorum call.

> The number of football injuries is *comparatively* high this year.

Relative to or compared with what?

QUALIFIERS: HEDGE IF YOU MUST

Qualifiers are necessary in statements open to doubt. Because news reports are often based on partial information, some hedging is inevitable: *possibly, perhaps, probably, allegedly, reportedly, on the whole* and so on.

Some writers are so addicted to using qualifiers—or so insecure—that they guard their flanks with such words even when the flanks need no guarding.

Dingell, it can *probably* be said with *absolute certainty* ...

Either *probably* or *absolute certainty* can be used, but not both.

Both men pleaded guilty to the *alleged* theft of $40,000.

Since they pleaded guilty, *alleged* is unneeded.

Patrons at the restaurant told police the *suspect* had methodically relieved them of their wallets and valuables. He then *allegedly* took the contents of the cash register and escaped through a side door.

Since the robber is not named, both *allegedly* and *suspect* are unnecessary, unless the writer suspected the victims of hallucinating.

Here's a case of a modifier, itself unnecessary, qualified into never-never land:

Saudi Arabia's *almost* single-minded obsession with security ...

An obsession implies single-mindedness. You're either single-minded or you aren't. If the writer suspected his assertion, he should have made the noun *preoccupation* and scuttled the adjective and adverb.

And here, an excessively timid writer is stuck in a qualifier that attacks the nervous system:

It certainly seemed that way in Belgrade, which had its worst night of bombing, coupled with a presumably unrelated earthquake at about 5:30 a.m.

"Presumably"? Could NATO have arranged that quake?

Look hard at *basically, essentially, fundamentally* and *company*, which are usually superfluous.

Basically, Sears is changing its price policy.

In a news story, you're not expected to give every aspect of the company's plan. If what you left out is important, put it in. If not, forget the qualifier.

They are called something else here, but *essentially* they work as security guards.

If that's what they do essentially, good enough:

In *simplest terms*, the heart acts like a pump.

That may imply to touchy readers that they couldn't follow you if you let yourself go. Anyway, you're supposed to write in simplest (but not oversimplified) terms.

Potential and *possible* often seem pointless.

> City negotiators are trying to head off a *possible* strike by teachers next week ...

They want to prevent a real strike, not a possible one.

> The intention is to discourage *potential* attacks against oil installations.

They want to discourage the genuine article.

Arguably, now popular, is usually meaningless. Anyone who spends time on the internet knows most anything is arguable.

> Leonard Bernstein was *arguably* one of the most dazzling musicians America has produced.

Make it *perhaps* or *probably*. Or better yet, find someone to whom you can attribute that opinion.

PUT VERBS TO WORK

The verb, particularly in the active voice, is ringmaster of the sentence. It sets pace and movement. A peculiarity of abstract writing is an aversion to strong verbs, which are thinned out into combinations of weak verb, abstract noun and modifier.

In the following sentences, the revision on the right shows the magic of verbs properly used:

The refugees *experienced severe hunger* in their wilderness retreat.	The refugees starved in their wilderness retreat.
Portland *showed a collective grief* over the deaths of the young climbers.	Portland grieved over the deaths of the young climbers.

Other symptoms of noun disease:

determined the truth of	verified
established conclusive evidence	proved
gave permission	permitted
held a meeting	met
reached an agreement	agreed
submitted his resignation	resigned
take into consideration	consider
take into custody	arrest, seize

Occasionally, the wordier form is justified to capture a nuance. *Reach an agreement* suggests a longer effort, perhaps, than *agree*. Usually, however, the single verb will do.

Effect and *impact* devour more precise verbs:

Teachers as well as parents have much *impact* on students' career choices.	... influence students' career choices.
The boycott had no *effect* on sales.	... did not reduce sales.
The prosecutor's statement had an obvious *effect* on the jury.	... swayed the jury.

We use *effect* and *impact* when we want to say something mattered without saying how it mattered. They tell us about the story rather than telling us the story.

BE SHORT, FAMILIAR, SPECIFIC

From what we have seen about clutter, vagueness and officialese, certain precepts arise. They were derived long ago from the practice of good writers. Consider them a charm against the legion of devils that forever try to turn prose into slush:

- Prefer the short word to the long.
- Prefer the familiar word to the fancy.
- Prefer the specific word to the abstract.
- Use no more words than necessary to make your meaning clear.

This does not mean that long or unfamiliar words should never be used. Sometimes, they fit the meaning best. Occasionally, they serve the rhythm of a sentence. But there must be good reasons for the choice. It's hard to see much advantage to long words such as those in the left-hand column:

accommodations	rooms
ameliorate	improve
approximately	about
assistance	help
commence	begin
deactivate	close, shut off
endeavor	try
finalize	end, complete

implement	carry out
in consequence of	because
initiate	begin
methodology	method
motivation	motive
objective	aim, goal
peruse	read
prior to	before
proliferation	spread
purchase	buy
reference	refer
remuneration	pay
replicate	repeat
socialize	mingle, meet, make friends
substantial proportion	many, much
underprivileged	poor
utilize	use

CORRAL THOSE MODIFIERS

The language has many ways to trip you up, most deviously through a modifier that turns up in the wrong place. Don't let related ideas in a sentence drift apart. Modifiers should be close to the word they modify, and verbs should be close to their subject.

> Gorbachev was last seen in public Aug. 7, when he received a group of U.S. teachers of the Russian language in Moscow.

They may have been hard up over there, but Russian they knew. (... *seen in public in Moscow Aug. 7* ...)

> Police hope an autopsy will confirm the identity of a teen-age boy whose body they found stuffed into a septic tank with the help of a self-proclaimed clairvoyant.

Sounds like the clairvoyant had a head start here. (... *whose body they found in a septic tank* ...) Stuff it later.

> A 6-year-old dog named Rosie has been honored by the American Humane Association for saving the life of her iron lung bound owner during a power outage with gifts of plaques and flowers and all the dog biscuits she could eat.

That must have done the patient a wealth of good.

> A Harlem man who disappeared a month ago was found slain by his wife in the trunk of the couple's car, police said.

Um, did she do it or not? "A Harlem woman found the body of her slain husband in the trunk of their car, police said. He disappeared a month ago." And those infamous dangling participles still claim victims:

> While eating dinner in a hotel restaurant later, a boyish-looking, pink-skinned man with premature gray hair and dressed in a blue jump suit bounded up to the table.

Interesting, but poor for the digestion.

> Already wheezing and short of breath, the principles of sound mountaineering were forgotten as they began their retreat.

As well they might be.

WHO'S WHO?

Pronoun pain ensues from placement that leaves the antecedent in doubt:

> He said he is certain it's an original de Torres painting, worth $200,000. The artist's signature is on it and it includes the faces of his favorite models, he said.

The pronoun *it* refers to *painting*, not the signature, which would have been worth $200,000 by itself with all those faces in it. Also, at first glance *he said* seems to refer to the dead artist, not the curator who was speaking.

> The foreman told reporters later the jurors had trouble believing the state's witnesses. "They were confused on most major points," he said.

They can be read as referring to the jury. Putting *witnesses* in brackets after *they* is not the best solution. Make it: *Their testimony "was confused on most major points," he said.*

THE ELEGANT VARIATION

Writers who believe that the repetition of plain words within shouting distance of each other is a crude take off on synonym safaris. The practice was long ago ridiculed by Fowler, who named it "elegant variation." It's all the more grotesque as there are few true synonyms and the author may introduce misfits:

> The mayor's task force was asked to meet with the owners of the structures, discuss whether they wanted their buildings preserved, and recommend ways to adapt older edifices to new use.

Structures could be anything and *edifices* is too grandiose; the story concerns commercial and apartment buildings.

If the writer didn't want to repeat *buildings*, a pronoun was the way out:

> ... to meet with the owners of the buildings, discuss whether they wanted them preserved, and recommend ways to adapt the older ones to new uses.

The same craving for daintiness will convert elephants to *pachyderms*, dogs to *canines*, cats to *felines*, tigers to *striped predators* and cars to *vehicles*. Petroleum becomes *black gold*, snow becomes *white powder* (a justly forgotten poet once called it *"God's dandruff"*), a banana turns into *the elongated yellow fruit*.

The most common and perhaps most obnoxious form of the elegant variation consists of substitutions for a news subject's name. John Doe, president of Chapter 11 Bank, is reintroduced in successive paragraphs as *the ruddy-faced financier, the Hawaii native, the silver-haired executive* and *the no-nonsense banker*.

All those descriptions are trying to tell us things without really saying them. Write what you mean.

AVOID PALLING PASSIVES

Use the active voice whenever possible. *Police arrested John Smith* is shorter and crisper than *John Smith was arrested by police*. On many occasions, of course, news values dictate the passive form, in leads especially. If you were writing about your town's leading citizen, you'd make it *Mayor John Smith was arrested by Smithtown police today*.

In most cases, though, the passive is flabby, dropping the doer of a deed out of the picture. That's why officialese favors the passive mode. *It is believed* or *it is estimated* allows the estimator and the believer to vanish in the fog. This is news. We care who is doing what to whom.

Other things being equal, the passive almost always loses out to the active form:

Lighted candles were carried by most of the demonstrators in Prague, and elsewhere there were silent demonstrations by large crowds.	Most of the demonstrators carried lighted candles in Prague that night, and elsewhere large crowds also demonstrated silently.

Always distrust *there were* and *there is*, especially at the start of a sentence. There is usually—oops! You can usually find a better way. Forms of the verb *to be* offer little action. Saying that something exists is impressive for toddlers, not journalists.

There was no one in the group of bystanders who came to the victim's aid.	No one in the group of bystanders helped him.

A sentence should be emphatic. When possible, express even a negative in positive form:

The Legislature did not consider the governor's proposal.	The Legislature ignored the governor's proposal.
The company said not all absentees had no excuse.	The company said some absentees had excuses.

Some years ago, a specialist in the analysis of extortion notes and terrorist threats told an interviewer that a note that says "I will kill you" suggests the writer means business. "You will be killed," on the other hand, suggests that the writer may waver, lacking "sufficient commitment to identify himself as the agency of the threat."

MISMANAGED BACKGROUND

Badly placed background detail in a story often produces sentences with wildly disparate ideas. *Born in Detroit, he was an ardent stamp collector* is the kind of non sequitur one finds in many obituaries. The havoc caused by background material worked in without regard for logic and relevance is shown in the following passages from a second-day story on Elvis Presley's death.

The story goes back years, but it's such a classic of disheveled backgrounding that it's worth exhuming. Besides, you can show it to people who insist that Elvis is still alive, something the autopsy story seems to disprove.

The writer struggles to tell essentials of the singer's career within the framework of developing news, and some of the sentences flop around like beached fish:

> Dr. George Nichopulos, longtime physician to the swivel-hipped, throaty baritone who was known as the King of Rock 'n' Roll, said an autopsy revealed a constriction in one of the arteries to the heart, which restricted blood flow and brought on a heart attack.

Presley, whose recording of "Heartbreak Hotel" helped put him on top of the entertainment world 21 years ago, was discovered unconscious at Graceland in suburban Memphis Tuesday afternoon.

The doctor said attempts to revive Presley, who appeared in 31 films—including "Love Me Tender" and "Jailhouse Rock"—continued because of a slight chance that life still existed in his body.

In the next example, too, misplaced details interfere with the flow of thought. The story is about a man who survived a long fall when his parachute failed to open.

The son of a postal worker, Mongillo was living in Florida when he had his brush with death.

Mongillo, whose only income is $100 a month from a local welfare fund, said, "I was scared. I knew I was going to die."

The answer to such difficulties is to disengage and regroup. In the Presley story, the facts about his death, the resuscitation effort and the autopsy belong in one section of the story, the facts of his rise to fame, film credits and song hits in another. In the Mongillo story, a separate paragraph should have wrapped up his postal antecedents and poverty.

Where background details can be woven smoothly into the narrative, it's the preferred way. Where they chop up the story and the logic of individual sentences, it's best to present the material in a coherent paragraph or two at an appropriate place in the story.

Useful as the inverted pyramid is—and it is indispensable for fast-breaking stories— it presents a risk. The sequence of central events is sometimes left foggy. Readers are told what happened, but not always how or in what order. Careful writers will sort it out in a clear, chronological summary somewhere in the story after they have disposed of the main news points. Often, matters are left like this:

Wielding homemade knives, the inmates commandeered a milk truck, which they used to vault over a 25-foot wall, he said. The group then threw Molotov cocktails made with paint thinner at a guard tower and leaped from the top of the truck.

When did they vault? When did they leap?

In the following example, a simple sequence becomes twisted by needless *befores* and *afters*:

Last Wednesday, the 3-year-old monkey escaped from a backyard leash and bit a woman and her son after jumping into their passing car.

Last Wednesday, Columbo slipped his leash and escaped from Coleman's backyard.

Neighbor Debbie Jackson testified that, before the attack, the monkey was taunted by several youths who raced at it with bicycles and screamed.

A neighbor testified that screaming youngsters raced at Columbo with their bicycles. The frightened monkey jumped into a passing car and bit the driver and her son.

After the biting, Columbo climbed into a tree and descended only after a boy coaxed him down with sliced bananas.

Columbo then climbed into a tree and stayed there until a boy coaxed him down with a banana.

Clean-and-lean sentences flourish best in a well-organized story. Mishandling of background gums up the machinery. That is largely a matter of organization. Jumping back and forth results in excess wordage and tires the reader. Complete each topic before going on to the next.

In structure and sentence: Simplify. Avoid clutter. Prune. Think twice.

Chapter 3

Leads: The Agony of Square One

In the beginning of every news story is the lead—the bait, the lure, the tender trap for the reader, a source of much fear and loathing for the writer.

Like a fiddle string, a good lead is the product of the right tension. Or, to get the metaphors out of the way, the lead is an hors d'oeuvre, intended to whet the appetite, not to provide a three-course dinner.

Don't be intimidated by leads, however. Do think of them as though they cost you 10 bucks per word, or as if each word were to be engraved on stainless steel while you're sitting on a hot stove. Think economy.

A good lead makes a clear statement of the essential news point and when possible includes a detail that distinguishes the story from others of its kind. If the bank robbers escaped in a baby blue Mercedes, that small fact belongs in the lead.

Leads should be clear and specific; they must not mumble. Mumblers stem from various defects:

- A gaggle of secondary detail

- Abstract and general language

- Mindreading, either the reader or the source

- Vagueness

- A focus on process, rather than the news itself

- Stress on how something is announced rather than what is said, or on how the news originates rather than the news itself

- Entanglement in the chronology of an event

DON'T BURY THE NEWS

To avoid mumblers, the lead writer must first decide what the most important news is, which can be difficult in situations where much is happening. The following mammoth evades that rule and dooms itself:

> WASHINGTON—Sen. Dave Durenberger, acknowledging that depositions in the ethics case against him appear to support key allegations, has canceled a 10-day trip to Moscow because of time spent on what he insists will be a strong defense to present to the Senate Ethics Committee.

Well, what's most important here? The cancellation of the trip? The acknowledgment?

The bit about the strong defense? If everything is important, then nothing is. The lead is about making choices.

Two of several possibilities:

> WASHINGTON—Sen. Dave Durenberger has canceled a 10-day trip to Moscow because of the time consumed by preparations for his defense in an ethics case.

> Sen. Dave Durenberger has acknowledged that depositions in the ethics case against him appear to support key allegations but says he will have a strong defense.

The next lead takes a long scenic route and smothers the news beneath 47 words and a colon.

> In a landmark legal case that took the emotional right-to-die issue from a snowy country road in rural Missouri to the halls of the Supreme Court in Washington, a county probate judge issued what is likely to be the final ruling in the matter yesterday: he authorized the family of Nancy Beth Cruzan to stop having chemical nutrition and water pumped into the comatose woman's stomach.

This gets to the point more quickly:

> A county probate judge in Missouri authorized the family of Nancy Beth Cruzan yesterday to discontinue medical intervention and allow her to die after seven years in an irreversible coma and a long legal battle.

Here's a lead that starts out strongly enough but fades near the end:

> The City Council has passed a law banning families with children aged 14 or under from certain parts of town.

Certain parts? Care to say which? Near the old swimming hole perhaps? Well, the answer is these families are banned from living near residential communities for senior citizens, and that's what the lead should have specified, along with other material found later in the story:

> Landlords in senior citizens' communities who sell or rent to families with young children face jail terms and fines under an ordinance passed by the City Council.

Here is a terminal mumbler. Only one word has a semblance of news interest, and it is hard to spot amid the debris:

> Rep. Ken Hechler, D-W.Va., said a decision Wednesday by the U.S. Court of Appeals that gives the go-ahead for the construction of the Blue Ridge power project on the New River is "ridiculous."

Just clearing away the clutter couldn't salvage that opener. You have to exhume an angle from the next-to-last graf of the story:

> Rep. Ken Hechler says people in West Virginia and two other states will mobilize to protect the New River after Wednesday's "ridiculous" court decision approving the Blue Ridge power project.

TOO MUCH, TOO LITTLE

Following are some typical leads, long and short, that say too much. A trimmed version is on the right.

WASHINGTON—The Federal Trade Commission agreed Friday to allow the nation's biggest leveraged buyout to go through, provided the two corporations involved—which together account for one-eighth of the food sold in the nation's supermarkets—reduce their share of the markets for ketchup, Oriental foods and packaged nuts.

WASHINGTON—The Federal Trade Commission agreed Friday to let the nation's biggest leveraged buyout go through if both corporations reduce their market share in ketchup, Oriental foods and packaged nuts.

PALM BEACH, Fla.—Israel remains America's most reliable ally in the world, but it must recognize that the killing of Palestinian civilians in the strife-torn West Bank and Gaza Strip is "clearly unacceptable," Vice President Dan Quayle told a Jewish group today.

PALM BEACH, Fla.—Israel remains the most reliable U.S. ally but must recognize that the killing of Palestinian civilians is "clearly unacceptable," Vice President Dan Quayle told a Jewish group today.

DALLAS—Mary Kay Cosmetics says it has placed a moratorium on using animals to verify the safety of its products.

DALLAS—Mary Kay Cosmetics says it has halted using animals to test product safety.

WASHINGTON—A fighter plane that combines long-range supersonic cruise capability with greatly enhanced ability to dogfight at and above the speed of sound has long been an elusive dream of aircraft engineers.

WASHINGTON—A supersonic plane built for long-range cruising and dogfights has long been a dream of aircraft designers.

The original carries a lethal dose of Pentagon jargon. And a long-held dream can't be anything but elusive.

The pruning knife is the remedy for verbose mumblers. There's no known cure for leads that say too little:

Gov. Mario Cuomo and his three opponents each view the crime issue—the biggest concern of voters, according to polls—in different ways.

Stop the presses; political candidates disagree on an issue.

ODON, Ind.—Vice Adm. John Poindexter's hometown was quiet Saturday night after his conviction on charges of conspiracy, obstruction and lying to Congress.

Did we expect riots or parades?

MINOCQUA, Wis.—What can you do when a tornado has flattened much of an eight-year dream, killing one person and leaving a twisted shambles where your resort and North woods campground had been?

People read the news to get answers, not more questions.

TRY WRITING "VISUALLY"

You can avoid mumblers by being specific and concrete, giving the reader a picture. A clever phrase, a touch of humor, and an ironic contrast help.

MADISON, Wis. (AP)—State Sen. Clifford "Tiny" Krueger eased his 300-pound frame into a witness chair Friday and said fat people should not be barred from adopting children.

That little gem draws the reader right into the story. The next tells virtually a whole story in two short sentences:

MIAMI (AP)—Bill Cashman, a fireman, says he didn't mind posing nude for a centerfold in a magazine for women who like men. But he has a $2 million objection to use of the picture by a magazine for men who like men.

It would be hard to stop reading here—as it would be after the following:

MARIETTA, Ohio (AP)—His work done, his children grown, his age past 80, his days of toil to get ahead well behind, George Oafkes nonetheless sat down one day and built a better mousetrap.

Next, a short lead (proving it doesn't take a lot of words to be effective).

BOSTON (AP)—Here's an insight that may fail to shock dedicated students of the mating game: People often tell lies in order to have sex.

This dealt with one of those sociological studies that tell you what you've known all your life.

BEIJING—China's decade-long shopping spree is over for now, squelched by a government austerity program that has pushed the nation precariously close to recession.

Homely language for complex economic developments. Even the shortest, simplest sort of lead can provide an alluring gateway, as the following from *USA Today* shows. It's about voters across the country turning down expensive programs:

If it cost money, Tuesday's voters weren't buying.

WHAT'S THE DIFFERENCE?

The real key to lifting your lead out of the humdrum is to ask yourself what is *different* about each story.

Much of the news is repetitive: war, crime, disaster. News, however, is meant to reveal the unusual. The goal, both in the lead and in the rest of the story, is to stress those angles that are least like those about similar events or issues. Often, writers focus on the routine, which means they overlook opportunities to provide their lead with that small hook that grabs the reader.

> A car sliced through a crowded fast food restaurant at lunchtime Tuesday, officials said, killing two people and injuring six others.

Nothing wrong with that lead. Well, perhaps the attribution, *officials said*, could wait until the second paragraph since nothing in the story is in contention. In any case, a car smashing into a restaurant at lunchtime is news enough for a lead, you might say, and it is written clearly and succinctly.

But eight grafs into the story appears a tidbit of information from the coroner. The two killed were a husband and wife, ages 72 and 68, who had stopped "to have a sandwich before going to the funeral home down the street for the funeral of their son-in-law's uncle." Aha, the writer should have said, and written:

> YOUNGSTOWN, Ohio—A car sliced through a fast food restaurant Tuesday, killing an elderly couple who had stopped for lunch on the way to a family member's funeral. Six other people were injured.

Alert writers and editors will constantly watch for such distinctive particulars. But note that this lead does not try to be too clever. It is a respectful news lead that acknowledges the particulars of a tragic story. Let the online trolls do the snark. More examples:

A report from New Zealand about a crazed shooter who killed 12 people in a remote town is dramatic enough, but down in the fourth graf the story gave the population as 28 souls. The fact that the killer wiped out nearly half the population should have been in the lead.

> SAN FRANCISCO—Children as young as 3 years old were found working in violation of child-labor laws, the U.S. Department of Labor said.

Unaccountably deferred was a striking particular: They were found working in an onion field.

This lead came to AP's New York General Desk:

DENVER—About 150 soot-covered firefighters made headway Monday in curbing the spread of a fire burning 1.6 million gallons of jet fuel at a tank near Stapleton International Airport.

The editor found a small, glittering fact in the copy and revised:

DENVER—Patience, and a quarter of the water that Denver uses in one day, enabled firefighters to rein in a fire ...

Sometimes a clever idea makes all the difference:

FRANKFORT, Ky. (AP)—Local school boards in Kentucky are being caught in the middle of a controversy over posting copies of the Ten Commandments in public school classrooms.

When the story arrived at the AP's General Desk in New York, the lead was reshaped this way, taking advantage of a blessed opportunity:

FRANKFORT, Ky. (AP)—Thou shalt post the Ten Commandments on the classroom wall, says a 1978 Kentucky law. Thou shalt not, says the U.S. Supreme Court. Help! say confused local school boards.

Needless to say, cleverness demands caution. It is easy to slip over the line into the sophomoric.

HARTFORD, Conn.—Hello, tree. There is good news and there is bad news for you today.

That's plain silly.

ACTION SPEAKS LOUDER

The more action your lead conveys, the better. Strong verbs are important.

Verbs like *moved*, *scheduled*, *expected*, and *prepared*, which so often crop up in second-day leads, are crutches. See what a good choice of verbs does for these leads:

NEW YORK—To the last day, Americans *flocked* to the tall ships at berth, *clambered up* the treacherous gangplanks, *grasped* the huge wheels, and *fondled* the brass windlasses.

FRANKLINTON, La.—A tank truck carrying 7,000 gallons of gasoline *collided* with a car and *overturned* Monday, crushing the trucker to death and igniting a fire that *spread* 50-foot flames over two blocks.

Following are three leads on the same subject. The first is pretty flat, relying on *linked* and ending lamely with *will result* ...:

> LONDON—Drillers working deep beneath the English Channel last night linked mainland Europe to Britain with a 2-inch-wide borehole that *will result* in a channel tunnel.

The second, by referring to the Ice Age, adds some color:

> LONDON—Eight thousand years after the Ice Age put them asunder, Britain and France were *reunited* Tuesday beneath the English Channel.

But *reunited* is abstract and feeble. And were they really? Despite its length—and maybe in this case because of it—the third lead is a success: *mud-caked* and the list of previous failures give a nice twist to the phrase after the dash.

> LONDON—A handful of mud-caked drillers working deep beneath the English Channel tonight succeeded where the Spanish Armada, Napoleon, Hitler and a small army of European Community bureaucrats all have tried and failed—they linked Britain to mainland Europe.

PITFALLS OF ATTRIBUTION

A common pitfall for the lead writer comes with attribution. We need to tell the readers where the information we report comes from. They need that to evaluate the news. That said, cattle may chew cud contentedly, but readers shouldn't be asked to digest the same bit of information several times within a few paragraphs. Such repetition is often due to clumsy structure, particularly in backing up or elaborating on the lead. Some writers have trouble introducing a new fact without swaddling it in information or phrases that have gone before. Double-decker leads result, the second or third graf saying much the same as the first.

Quotes are a requirement, but they need to add something to a story. If you can say it better as a paraphrase, the quotes are probably not that strong. When you back up your lead with repetitive quotes, your entire story weakens.

The most common misstep is using quotes that largely repeat what the lead has already told us:

> LUBBOCK, Texas—School district officials were surprised by a judge's restraining order on the district's dress code, which allows boys with long hair and earrings to return to classes.

"We were somewhat surprised," said Mike Moses, superintendent of the Lubbock Independent School District.

WASHINGTON—The U.S. government is requiring some French and Italian vineyards to certify that wines imported by this country do not contain traces of a fungicide not approved in the United States.

"*We* have found a little bit of Italian wine and some French wine that contain traces of a fungicide not approved in the United States," Food and Drug Administration spokesman Bill Grigg said Sunday.

Another vintage double-decker:

Half of the Philadelphia Art Museum's permanent galleries were closed Sunday because of a shortage of security guards.

Museum officials said they had to close part of the museum because the city had not provided money for about 100 additional guards.

In attributing and getting to the 100 guards, half the lead is repeated. Slight recasting moves the story along:

Half of the Philadelphia Art Museum's permanent galleries were closed Sunday because the city had failed to provide money for 100 more security guards, Director Edward Turner said.

Attribute we must, but when information is not controversial, the source can sometimes wait until the second paragraph:

PHILADELPHIA—Former Defense Secretary Frank C. Carlucci has been elected to Bell Atlantic's board of directors.

This information is likely the result of a Bell Atlantic press release. Unless the election is being contested, this declarative statement is probably safe.

By contrast, instant attribution was mandatory in the following lead. The writer couldn't be sure the secret talks had taken place:

SEOUL, South Korea—South Korea and North Korea have held secret talks on improving relations and discussed a possible meeting between their leaders, newspaper reports said today.

If the attribution is in the lead, often it appears at the end of the sentence, like this. The news of the meeting is the reason for writing the story. Where you found it is important, but secondary.

HORSE FIRST, THEN CART

Far too many leads are wounded by starting out with a long subsidiary clause that marches ahead of the main idea. That procedure usually buries the action. An added reason for suspicion: You never hear that kind of a sentence in conversation.

Let's wheel in our first patient, barely breathing:

> Declaring it "is in the best interests of science and the American and French people," U.S. officials ended a decade-long dispute by according French researchers the lion's share of the millions of dollars in patent royalties produced by the sales of the AIDS blood test.

The initial clause, with its fatuous rhetoric, sprawls over the substance—what was done—like an avalanche over a skier. Start with the action because that is the fact rather than the analysis. Demote the opening clause to the second paragraph (if you need it at all):

> U.S. officials ended a decade-long dispute by awarding French researchers a lion's share of the millions of dollars in patent royalties from sales of the AIDS blood test.

> They said the settlement was "in the best interests ..."

There's not enough news for burial here, but you can still help:

> Describing himself as rejuvenated in the two years since he left the Senate and now "on top of his game," Bradley, 55, said he believed he could offer the leadership necessary to address the nation's problems—from the lack of affordable health care insurance to childhood poverty.

Convert the subsidiary clause into a direct statement and break the lead into two sentences. It won't be more interesting, but at least it will sound more natural:

> Bradley described himself as rejuvenated in the two years since he left the Senate and now "on top of my game." He said he believed he could offer the leadership needed to deal with the nation's problems, from the lack of affordable health insurance to childhood poverty.

The subsidiary clause vanishes, and we get two manageable—and even pronounceable— sentences of 21 and 26 words. And we clean up the misquoted "on top of *his* game."

A short introductory phrase, on the other hand, is often effective:

> One wing afire, an Air Force plane made a successful emergency landing at ...

The test is simple: Does the phrase help what follows or just get in the way?

Another disruptive formula starts the lead with the subject, then meanders off into a dependent clause before getting to the verb and the news:

> WASHINGTON—President Clinton, saying that Mexico had cooperated fully in the war on drugs, plans to take up trade matters with Mexican officials in the near future.

Often, there's sound reason for starting a lead with the source, notably when the statement or action derives all its significance from the speaker or doer. Not much reason here, however:

> WASHINGTON—The General Accounting Office, an investigative branch of Congress, issued a report Tuesday recommending federal leadership ...

Yes, yes, but what did it say?

> ... to reduce the amount of low-level radioactive waste from nuclear plants.

SECOND-CYCLE WOES

Overstuffing, double-decking and other fatal diseases are often encountered when the writer is struggling with that old nemesis, the second-cycle lead. Every reporter will eventually confront a second-cycle lead; for Associated Press reporters, it is a part of the daily routine. Since phrases like "day before yesterday" are not in the vocabulary of leads, the problem arises in trying to make old news appear fresh. With no new development to come to the rescue, writers are left to their own resources.

Minimally, the second-cycle lead should cannibalize the first report for a different angle to stress.

An AM story, for example, led with a bankruptcy judge's approval of $135 million in cash so Eastern Air Lines could keep flying through the winter. The PM version led with a statement by the airline's trustee, which was subordinated in the original, that the cash infusion would be enough to help the carrier return to profitability.

The following second-day lead took a feature angle:

> DILLINGHAM, Alaska—No matter how they voted in yesterday's election, some residents of the Bristol Bay region were sure to wind up with a turkey.

(A reward for the village with the highest turnout.) And another fresh approach on the day after a fire:

> UNIVERSAL CITY, Calif. (AP)—Hollywood tourists took a closeup look at a scene of destruction requiring no special effects: the gutting of the Universal Studios backlot.
>
> Trams full of visitors rolled past smoldering remains ...

This writer settled for the routine:

> LAS VEGAS, Nev.—Arson investigators sifted through the rubble of a spectacular fire Sunday that leveled most of a shopping center just off the heart of the glittering Las Vegas strip.
>
> The blaze that began Saturday night destroyed ...

Leads that report investigators (or grim-faced rescue workers, or weary homeowners) *sifting through the rubble* or *poking through the debris* are written by writers wallowing in clichés. A narrative or anecdotal lead would be more interesting than one describing those overworked rescue workers in disaster stories: *Most families in Smithtown were having supper when the sirens sounded. In the next few minutes ...*

No fresh developments here, but the writer came up with an interesting angle by adding things up:

> SAN RAFAEL, Calif.—The state of California spent 16 months and more than $2 million to convict three men who were already imprisoned, two with life sentences. Three of the San Quentin Six were found guilty Thursday ...

That lead was written at the end of a trial. Reporters covering the early stages of a trial face tougher problems. Trials have moments of high drama, but the phase of jury selection is not among them. Yawning reporters often refer to it as the *long, tedious process* of seating a jury, but the process is far from tedious to lawyers and defendants, whose minds are on other matters than providing entertainment.

Terrible leads are often written during that phase: *Three more jurors were tentatively seated Thursday as the trial entered its fifth day,* which is later topped with a lead that has two more jurors chosen.

Obviously, the number of jurors chosen must be reported. Probably the best way to handle it is to mention high up that jury selection is continuing, and then, in the middle of your story, run a paragraph that by such and such a time X number of jurors had been picked. You can update the figures without changing the lead or breaking the continuity of the story. Meantime, work on a more interesting angle. For example:

MINEOLA, N.Y. (AP)—Prospective jurors in the trial of a doctor charged with the "mercy killing" of a dying cancer patient were closely questioned about their religious beliefs and attitudes toward the medical profession.

This second-day lead makes a significant point. The numbers (*Eight jurors have been seated ...*) fell into place later in the story.

WATCH THE BOUNCING BALL

While on the subject of covering the courts, beware another snare in this special field of reporting. Court rulings, administrative decisions and the like are usually couched in technicalities and legalese, and leads don't always simplify these terms the way they should. Here's an example:

A federal judge refused Wednesday to issue a temporary injunction halting a union ratification vote on the binding arbitration contract handed down last week for the American Postal Workers union and the U.S. Postal Service.

Anybody care to tell a struggling reader what happened? Well, it was like this. The judge wouldn't block the vote on a contract. Moreover, since the contract resulted from binding arbitration—meaning the union members weren't free to accept or reject it—the vote could have no effect. They were going through motions, that's all. So:

A federal judge on Wednesday let postal workers go ahead with the formalities of voting on a new contract imposed through binding arbitration.

AP President and former Executive Editor Lou Boccardi calls this turgidity in court coverage "tennis-ball writing." Here's another example:

WASHINGTON—The U.S. Court of Appeals agreed Wednesday to review a lower court order that found the Nuclear Regulatory Commission in contempt of court for violating an order to hold open budget meetings.

Boccardi's comment in his writing bulletin, Prose and Cons: "The problem here is that we treat the reader's mind like a tennis ball to be whacked back and forth across the net. Agreed to review. Bam! Contempt of court. Bam! For violating an order. Bam! To hold open meetings. Bam! You can almost see the ball flying back and forth. It's just too much. You cure it by just stepping back and asking yourself, 'What really happened here?'"

This happened:

> WASHINGTON—The U.S. Court of Appeals agreed Wednesday to review a contempt finding against the Nuclear Regulatory Commission for holding a closed meeting.

And this isn't perfect. *Contempt* is a legal term with a specific meaning that readers may not share. Reporters indulge in tennis-ball writing and legal jargon because they don't quite trust themselves to tell in a straightforward way what's going on. By sticking to the legal terms, they play it safe. Here's an example of playing it so safe the story is unintelligible:

> RICHMOND, Va.—Attorney General Andrew P. Miller says a juvenile who in a juvenile or domestic relations court is convicted of and receives a sentence for what, if committed by an adult, would be a misdemeanor or a felony cannot be housed with adult prisoners in prisons or jails.
>
> In an opinion released Monday, Miller said it would be a violation of state law to incarcerate juveniles in such a manner unless the incarceration is mainly for the purpose of pre-trial detention or if the juvenile is certified to a circuit court and tried as an adult.

That's a legal tennis match to boggle the mind. In English, I presume it would mean this:

> RICHMOND, Va.—A youthful offender receiving a prison sentence in a juvenile or domestic relations court cannot be jailed with adult prisoners, the attorney general has ruled.
>
> Placing him with adult inmates would violate state law unless it's for pre-trial detention or he has been tried in a circuit court.

LEGALISTIC LEADS

Sometimes—and this is true on the cops and courts beat especially—we need legalistic words and phrases to account for uncertainty. One of these is *in connection with* when used in stories about people who are questioned or arrested or sought for a crime with which they haven't been charged. But there's absolutely no warrant for using it *after* a man has been charged (say what he was charged with) or after he's been sentenced or pronounced guilty. Some reporters are so afflicted with the legal shakes that you can read:

> Joseph Smith was scheduled Monday to be sentenced in connection with the Smithtown murder after a jury convicted him ...

A jury verdict is a finding of fact (even if the jury turns out to be wrong later). But this is fine too:

> Joseph Smith will be sentenced Monday after a jury convicted him in the Smithtown murder case.

Another abused word is *suspect*. It's seldom a very good word to use in any case; if somebody is questioned, or wanted for questioning, let those facts speak for themselves. If the authorities declare somebody to be *a prime suspect* in a case, so be it; quote them. It is ridiculous in crime stories, however, to refer to unknown but indubitable culprits as *suspects*. While nobody knows their names, they're the ones who have done it:

> Two suspects held up a jewelry store at 14th and Main today, tying up a clerk and rifling several display cases before escaping.

Provide a detail that makes these suspects unique, perhaps.

THE TIME ELEMENT

A special problem with leads is comparatively recent: the shift to the use of the day of the week. *Today* and *yesterday* fit gracefully into leads. *Thursday* and *Friday* are often balky.

As a rule, put the time element after the verb unless the day of the week can be read as the object of the verb or is awkward in other ways, producing oddities. A Washington story reports that Congress *postponed Wednesday*. (Talk about big government!) In New York, a top federal mediator *sought Thursday*, presumably without finding it. A story begins, *Middlesex Superior Court Judge Henry Chielinsky Thursday ...*

Some writers stick *on* before the day, interrupting the succession of capital letters, but this is generally considered a nonsolution, adding a word with little gain.

There's no ready formula. You must use your ear as well as your eye. How does it sound? Some leads read well with the day of the week, others don't. When it's cumbersome no matter where you try to shoehorn the word into a sentence, drop the day to the second paragraph, where it often fits quite naturally. You do *not* have to put the time element in every lead, either AMs or PMs.

Wrestling with such small details, and with many larger matters of technique, may be joyless, but in leads every word must count. Some of my editing of clumsy leads cited earlier doubtless could be improved further. The direction in any case should be clear: toward a lean, uncluttered sentence, toward the news itself rather than byplay, toward logical order of thought, toward concrete and specific language. Those are the lead writer's goals.

Chapter 4

The Case for the Period

Sentences come under special strains in news writing. A lot of facts have to be squeezed into a tight space; afterthoughts are often accommodated in haste. There's a tendency to overload sentences and let them swell to unseemly length.

But the longer the sentence, the less readable it's likely to be, and the more exposed to mishaps of syntax. The remedy is simple: Chop up long sentences into their functional components and aim for an average sentence length of 16 to 17 words. Happily for those writing in the internet age, clarity aligns with the desires of the search engines.

Note that I say "average." We don't want all sentences to be that short; you'd be writing kindergarten stuff. But the average gives you leeway for a comely mixture; it lets short sentences predominate, relieved by occasional longer ones. Variety of sentence structure further ensures against monotony.

There are no absolute rules of good writing—generalizations are instantly riddled with exceptions—**but the principle of the 16-word average comes closest.** No other single principle you can follow will yield such quick results in clarity and vigor.

Short sentences are not for everyone. They worked splendidly for Hemingway, as they work for Annie Dillard today. They worked for James Joyce in *Dubliners*—never mind *Finnegans Wake*—but you won't find many in Melville or Faulkner.

It's not necessary that every passage in every story meet the brevity standard, though all stories should approximate it as a whole. Whenever the average sentence length climbs to 20 words or more, many readers are in trouble.

Long, complicated sentences present no obstacle to professional readers (like ourselves). But we don't write for professional readers. And even they prefer the tighter prose that a preponderance of short, declarative sentences creates.

The bright side here is that sentence length is rather simple to control. The period mark, in lieu of all those conjunctions, participial and relative clauses, is a splendid antidote. Some of us need to rediscover it.

First aid, not major surgery, is usually all that's needed. Let's see how it works with sentences of the kind that often lure writers into quicksand.

A good way to deflate sentences stuffed with relative clauses is to use pronouns whenever they offer a smooth alternative.

> Cabinet ministers, leading politicians and foreign envoys were caught up in the melee that erupted moments after President Daniel arap Moi left the grounds of the Valley Road Pentecostal Church in his official limousine.

> Thousands of people had gathered outside the church, about a mile from downtown Nairobi, for the service of Robert Ouko, whose charred body was found with a bullet hole through the skull near his farm in western Kenya on Feb. 16.

Break up those sentences of 34 and 41 words and you come up with 13, 20, 20 and 21:

> Cabinet ministers, leading politicians and foreign envoys were caught up in the melee. It erupted moments after President Daniel arap Moi left the grounds of the Valley Road Pentecostal Church in his limousine.

> Thousands of people had gathered outside the church, about a mile from downtown Nairobi, for the service for Robert Ouko. His charred body was found with a bullet hole through his skull near his farm in western Kenya on Feb. 16.

Sentences can often be shortened by getting rid of dependent clauses starting with *although, even though* and the like.

> But the commission led by Moakley said Wednesday that doubts remain as to whether the people who planned the slayings have been identified, even though a Salvadoran army colonel has been arrested.

Turn this around (and forget *as to whether*):

> A Salvadoran army colonel has been arrested. But the commission led by Moakley said Wednesday it's doubtful that the people who planned the slayings have been identified.

Avoid pointless prepositional phrases:

> Cheney said some 5,000 of the troops would be pulled out of South Korea, with an additional 7,000 to 9,400 being withdrawn from the Philippines, officials said.

Instead, use two sentences:

> Cheney said some 5,000 of the troops would be pulled out of South Korea. An additional 7,000 to 9,400 would be withdrawn from the Philippines, officials said.

Guard against long dependent clauses and appositives:

> Those transfers, estimated by Selma's two all-white private schools to be as many as 35 in one day, included the sixth-grade son of white school board member Edie Jones, who enrolled Monday at all-white Morgan Academy in Selma.

That's 38 words. The underlined words are superfluous in the context. But let's unravel:

> Selma's two all-white private schools estimate that those transfers could have reached 35 in one day. One youngster, who enrolled in the sixth grade at Morgan Academy on Monday, is the son of white school board member Edie Jones.

We now have 16 and 22, respectively.

The next sentence, 33 words, cries out for a strategic period mark and slight rephrasing:

> But they said they would not attend classes as they pursued their demands for the retention of the city's first black superintendent, and for the placement of more black students in higher-level courses.

A more manageable version at 20 and 9:

> But they said they would skip classes to pursue their demands for retention of the city's first black school superintendent. They also want more black students in higher-level courses.

Next is a slightly different type of heavyweight, 39 words:

> The young Soviet state under Lenin's leadership confiscated most private property after the 1917 revolution and Stalin's drive to strip peasants of their land through collectivization in the 1930s claimed millions of lives through famine, deportation and summary execution.

You have two long independent clauses linked by a conjunction. Cut the link:

> The young Soviet state under Lenin's leadership confiscated private property after the 1917 revolution. Later, Stalin's drive to strip peasants of their land through collectivization in the 1930s claimed millions of lives through famine, deportation and summary execution.

Note the need for similar surgery in the following lead:

> WASHINGTON (AP)—Federal Reserve Chairman Alan Greenspan said today the economy has likely passed the danger point for an imminent recession, and he predicted continued, although modest, economic growth for the rest of this year.

End the lead sentence after *recession* and carry on with *He predicted continued* ....

The next example is a somewhat messy lead, but this time, the issue is a very long compound predicate:

> NEW YORK (AP)—Cable TV mogul Ted Turner urged advertisers to take the high road and keep in mind long-term interests in programs they sponsor, and accused the three largest networks of being more concerned with audience size than quality.

Substitute a pronoun for the second *and*:

> NEW YORK (AP)—Cable TV mogul Ted Turner urged advertisers to take the high road and keep in mind long-term interests in the programs they sponsor. He accused the three largest networks of being more concerned with audience size than quality.

This is still a bit much for a lead, but at least it's two sentences of 23 and 15 words each rather than one 37-word gulp.

When, after, as and similar crutches often prolong sentences needlessly:

> The company will not issue a general recall in its home country after a preliminary ruling by Health Ministry officials that it poses no public danger, Levin said.

Why not simply:

> The company will not issue a general recall in its home country. A preliminary ruling by Health Ministry officials found no danger to the public, Levin said.

Obviously, the ruling preceded the decision.

CHRISTOPHER, Ill. (AP)—The long-distance courtship of Toby the robot by an infatuated doll named Jodi ended just before Valentine's Day when Toby learned that Jodi had gone to the big doll house in the sky.

This good lead becomes crisper by deleting the *when*:

CHRISTOPHER, Ill. (AP)—The long-distance courtship of Toby the robot by an infatuated doll named Jodi ended just before Valentine's Day. Toby learned that Jodi had gone to the big doll house in the sky.

This sentence achieves 49 words:

"U.S. troops will remain in Korea as long as they are needed to guarantee the peace, and the Korean and American peoples and governments want them to remain," Cheney said after arriving from Hawaii on the first stop of a two-week tour of Asian nations hosting the U.S. forces.

Add a period after *Cheney said*. Continue with *He arrived from Hawaii* .... This 34-word graf is strengthened by dropping the conjunction.

While talks on reunification opened, another piece of the Cold War headed into oblivion as East German border guards started dismantling the Berlin Wall between the Reichstag building and the Checkpoint Charlie border crossing.

The initial *while* establishes the sequence; the *as* merely blunts the sentence.

While talks on reunification opened, another piece of the Cold War headed into oblivion. East German border guards started dismantling the Berlin Wall between the Reichstag building and the Checkpoint Charlie border crossing.

We're too fond of participial phrases that merely lengthen sentences and slow the pace:

The civil rights groups' national chairman, William F. Gibson of Greenville, S.C., announced the agreement with the Columbia Mall on Monday, saying it was the first pact reached with a shopping mall on the hiring and treatment of blacks.

That's 38 words. Add a period after *Monday*, followed by *He said* .... Another instance of eluding the period through a participial tail:

The presiding judge refused to tell jurors they could consider convicting the defendant only of bank larceny, saying that no reasonable juror could conclude that the tellers at each bank had handed him the money voluntarily rather than as a result of intimidation.

Add a period after *larceny* and follow with an independent sentence. This method almost always works.

Statistical material, bunches of figures and the like don't lend themselves very well to narrative form. They can become lethal when stuffed into a single sentence:

> Under the plan announced by Daniel S. Goldin, administrator of the National Aeronautics and Space Administration, the agency would cut about 28,000 Civil Service and contractor positions, restructure each of its 10 centers—several would lose 20 percent to 30 percent of their workers—and start a process that would eventually turn over the operations of the space shuttle program to private industry.

This isn't incomprehensible, but readers' eyes are bound to glaze over. You can break this monstrous 62-worder into four or five separate sentences. However, it's best to regroup and tighten as follows:

> Under the plan announced by Daniel S. Goldin, administrator of the National Aeronautics and Space Administration, the agency would:
>
> –Cut about 28,000 Civil Service and contractor positions.
>
> –Revamp all of its 10 centers. Some would lose 20 to 30 percent of their workers.
>
> –Eventually turn over its space shuttle program to private industry.

Like the original sentence, this isn't poetry, but it is much crisper and more readable. (Remember the useful format.)

Here's a routine bit of narrative, the sort where individual sentences usually spread like the oil slick they describe. In this case they are readable, because the sentence average is 15 words.

> When the leak stopped Thursday night, the Coast Guard began pumping the remaining oil and water from the compartment onto a barge. By 6 a.m. today, about 26,000 gallons had been transferred, said Lt. Cmdr. Alan Carver.
>
> Ten skimming boats worked on the slick, which covered water over an area roughly measuring 6 miles by 4 miles. Seas were calm and winds light.
>
> "The weather has cooperated," Carver said.
>
> Offshore winds Thursday had kept the slick away from beaches until afternoon, when they reversed direction and began nudging the mess onto shore. Pockets of crude oil began washing ashore Thursday night.
>
> A 4-mile stretch was fouled in Newport Beach, an affluent community that boasts some of Southern California's most expensive beachfront property.

A FEW LAST WORDS.../CONCLUSION (?)

That's how we write in our simple-and-direct mode, avoiding entanglements and convulsions. And it's the practice wherever clarity and readability are cherished.

That much-admired British weekly *The Economist* deals with heavy subjects, but the writing is light and bright. Many intros average 16 words. Most of the sentences hover between 16 and 19, usually at the low end of the scale. *The Economist* is not written for dummies.

Chapter 5

Journalese

Like the character from a Molière play who was astounded to learn that he'd been speaking prose all his life, many news writers might be surprised to hear that much of the time, they're writing journalese.

One would like to say that this sub-language is bush-league stuff, manufactured by raw novices at backwater weeklies. One would like to say it, but it isn't true.

Hardly any news organization is entirely free of the contagion, and even polished writers and prestigious publications will lapse occasionally. Nor can we blame invading bureaucratese and alien jargons. Journalese is our very own. The bacteria are nurtured in our professional culture. This enemy of sophisticated tone is us.

The plague goes back to the fossil strata of the profession, the era of drinkers and wanderers who loved to whoop it up and make great noise in their copy as in their lives, and didn't mind stretching a fact or two. In those days, for instance, every shipwreck story had a cat, which, if not accounted for in official reports, needed to be mentioned.

Those wild days are gone, but journalese still flourishes. If the facts are more accurate, the repetition of phrases is the new missing cat. New—if instantly old—terms have been added (*send a message, target, charisma*), but much of the old stock vocabulary remains in use (*crucial, ironic, historic, unique*).

It was over 50 years ago when Wilson Follett, in his *Modern American Usage*, explained the phenomenon:

> "In general, journalese is the tone of contrived excitement," he wrote. "When the facts by themselves do not make the reader's pulse beat faster,

the journalist thinks it is his duty to apply the spur and whip of breathless phrases. Since these exist only in finite numbers they get repeated, and repetition begets their weakening, their descent into journalese."

This underworld bears some examination for its power to transform gold into plastic by reverse alchemy.

Let's assume two ordinary mortals, neighbors, are discussing a recent disturbance in their suburb, and run their conversation through this process:

> SMITH: Joe, I'll note candidly that my concern has been escalating for weeks, and the latest incident has really fueled my ire. What's triggering a small but growing number of our area youths, who keep sparking confrontations down by our tranquil duck pond?

> JONES: They certainly shattered the stillness of the affluent neighborhood with their drug-related pre-dawn rampage. No wonder violence flared when the club-wielding police reached the turbulent scene. I understand the Doe youth had to be rushed to a nearby medical facility.

> SMITH: Yes, he is lingering in guarded condition. His mother is grief-stricken. But I am thankful that our usually soft-spoken, mild-mannered, pipe-puffing—not to say wimpy— mayor lashed out at the alleged suspects, vowing to curb future outbursts.

> JONES: He certainly fired off a clear signal. His move spawns some hope of resolving the problem.

This exchange doesn't exactly throb with the vigor of the American idiom. Nobody talks that way. But that's how news is too often written—in smaller blotches, true, but enough to drain the life from many a story.

Take the following passage:

> The president, whose wavering stance on the question of boosting taxes on the rich has sparked frustration and ridicule on Capitol Hill, has expressed confidence that a plan will be hammered together.

News copy isn't written for the ages, but this sentence has a shelf life of two seconds. It's mechanically "hammered together" from prefabricated phrases. Almost any version in plain English will be better:

> The president's changing positions on tax increases for the rich has stirred up annoyance and ridicule on Capitol Hill, but he says he is confident that something will be worked out.

The next example sounds like my parody:

> The 700-member union struck *The Daily News* last night, triggering a climactic labor confrontation with the management of the financially ailing paper.

Less shrill:

> The 700-member union struck *The Daily News* last night for the final showdown in a long, bitter labor dispute with the management of the paper. *The News* has been losing money for years.

None of this is extreme. You can pluck examples at random every day and see how easily you can rid your writing of journalese:

Tensions between Arizona's two senators flared before the Senate's ethics committee ...	Arizona's two senators quarreled openly before the Senate ethics committee ...
In a move aimed at increasing revenues, the airline is hiking its full coach fares—the unrestricted, widely available fares targeted toward business travelers.	Trying to increase revenues, the airline is raising its full coach fares—unrestricted, widely available fares intended for business travelers.
An immediate focus of concern is the United States' intention to break off dialogue ...	An immediate worry is the United States' intention to break off talks ...
President Mikhail Gorbachev yesterday won the Nobel Peace Prize for easing international tensions ...	President Mikhail Gorbachev yesterday won the Nobel Peace Prize for helping to end the Cold War ...
The thorny issue of free agency was brought into sharper focus ...	The thorny issue of free agency received fresh attention ...

A more elaborate example is the following story. It's dramatic and clearly told, but for writers of journalese, enough is never enough:

> A *blazing* fire broke out on the 47th floor of a Lower Manhattan skyscraper today, threatening to turn it into a *towering inferno*.
>
> Seven persons were injured—at least one critically—and two others were reported missing, the Fire Department said.
>
> Hundreds—many of whom had been eating in a *posh* restaurant—fled the building. Traffic on Lower Broadway was brought to a *complete* halt.

> An unidentified cleaning man who was riding the freight elevator was injured when the elevator opened on the 47th floor.

> Flames *exploded* and *blasted* him in the face.

> "His body was ignited head to foot," a witness said.

The fire is *blazing*, the restaurant *posh*, traffic comes to a *complete* halt, flames *explode* and *blast* AND ignite the man from head to foot. (And where was the witness? In the *inferno*, clad in asbestos?)

Enough journalese slides into news copy to multiply examples without great effort. We can quarrel over a word here and there and disagree whether a given context supports a supercharged term. But I doubt that there's much argument about the underlying distemper, those breathless words and phrases; the compulsion, for instance, to "ignite" a "wrenching debate" in Poland's presidential campaign because "wrenching" without ignition wouldn't be strong enough.

Writers of journalese chain themselves to the particular catchwords and clichés of their dialect. Explosions (always violent) must rip, earthquakes endlessly rock, spectacular fires sweep—often trapping victims as horrified spectators stand by helplessly.

Later, grim-faced rescue workers comb through smoldering rubble to the wails of grief-stricken relatives.

Politicians *lambaste, assail, rap* or *lash out at*; otherwise, they *craft legislation, policies* or *strategies*. Often they *vow*, never merely *promise, pledge* or *say*.

Police are *club-wielding*, assailants *knife-wielding*, troops *heavily armed*. Tempers, tensions and violence all *flare* (sometimes, embarrassingly, spelled *flair*). Dissidents *stalk*, never *walk*, from halls. Demonstrators *spark angry confrontations*. Rain doesn't fall but is *dumped* as rivers *rampage*.

Prices are *hiked* or *boosted*, hopes or enterprises are *spawned* (never mind that the verb relates to fish eggs) and nothing merely *starts*—it is *created* or *quickened*; things are *triggered, sparked* and *fueled*. In journalese, you can even read about a "chilling effect fueled by the court decision" in a libel case.

Heads of state and other public figures may still be hailed, as Julius Caesar was, but no longer do they *warn, hint, suggest* or *imply*. The secretary of state's speech *sends a message*. The White House *emits signals—clear, strong* or *mixed*. Egypt's president *signals the alarm of Arab countries with a surprise visit to two of them*. (*Surprise* usually signals a reporter's failure to get advance word.) When prosecutors indict the physician-inventor of a suicide machine, they do it to *send a clear message* to other would-be facilitators.

But why go on with the kind of stuff you'll be reading—though I hope not writing—tomorrow? Still, two more words, each used as verb and noun, deserve mention because they are so lavishly overused: *called for/ on* and *concern(ed)*. They've been turned into dimwitted predators, nosing into places where other, more specific words would serve better or at least offer relief from monotony.

President Bush calls for a budget compromise. The senator called on the two agencies to settle their feud. The administration bill calls for major revisions. All but forgotten in this unseemly bellowing are *urged, recommended, proposed, suggested, asked for, demanded* and *requested*, among other verbs.

Not surprisingly, a check of just the AP's national report for three weeks turned up *called for* and slight variants 347 times. Project that over a year, and you get nearly 10,000. Add newspapers' own usage, and we may reach 15,000 or more. That's overloading.

Concern, concerned and *express concern* are in wide general use and not typically journalese except for the overpowering monomania that expects a single bass fiddle to cover the range of an orchestra. It may be *the* word-of-all-trades, showing up 543 times in three weeks on the AP news report. Consider these examples:

> Wildlife groups are concerned (believe) that the busts point to a jump in poaching of pangolins.

> Officials were concerned (worried) that a twisted rail could break free and hurt someone.

> That requirement has drawn legality concerns (objections) because states can't deny free public education on the basis of immigration status.

> He was concerned about (sympathetic to) his aide's plight.

> The board refused because it was concerned about (objected to) taking on more debt.

> The community is determined to address the AIDS patients' concerns (needs).

When one general term eclipses so many meanings, precision is lost, and this is one way in which journalese sets its traps for the unwary and the negligent. Competent writers manage to avoid them, and it is they who account for the genuine quality of much of our journalism.

We cite the following story for its quality and style, and also because it has some historical significance. It was written when the old Yugoslavia was at the brink of dissolution; much of it had come about near the end of the millennium and to the sounds of NATO bombs.

You'll find no cliché-mongering in this *New York Times* story, no chatter about "escalating confrontations," "rising tensions throughout the embattled country" or "acute crises in the republics" and so on. Instead, readers get specifics, a cool assessment with excellent background and perspective.

> BELGRADE, Yugoslavia—Intensifying conflicts and rivalries among Yugoslavia's republics are bringing the country dangerously close to the breaking point, say people who favor the process as well as those who fear it.
>
> Nerves are fraying throughout the country. In Slovenia, the Government has deployed its own armed guards to underscore claims that the republic's sovereignty is paramount. In Croatia, gangs of heavily-armed Serbs have blocked roads in the enclaves where they are numerically strong. In Serbia's Kosovo region, ethnic Albanians speak openly of armed uprising. Travel from republic to republic, and the inventory of conflict grows.
>
> An international effort may soon be needed to head off a conflagration, Slovenia's Prime Minister, Lojze Peterie, said this week.
>
> A dream of 19th-century Slav Romantics, Yugoslavia is now a crumbling mosaic of peoples of Eastern Orthodox, Roman Catholic or Muslim traditions who have lived since World War II in a federation. Though conflicts and vendettas laced the region for years, for much of the postwar period national unity was advanced by a modicum of prosperity and the now-defunct Yugoslav Communist Party's monopoly, which muffled the quarrels.
>
> Much like the erosion of central power and rise of nationalist emotions in the Soviet Union, the breakdown of Communist-imposed unity and the emergence of democratic openness in Yugoslavia have released long-suppressed national aspirations, envies and antagonisms.

This is sober, effective news writing, without trumpets blaring, metaphors clashing and harlequins yodeling. The words both tell and show, and there's never a shriek.

Journalese in its overemphatic mode is like the Great Dane that's never outgrown its puppyhood and leaps up at his owner's cringing guests to beslobber their faces. It's one way to get attention, but not the best.

Even more coldly put, journalese means hack work. To write well means to choose the right words for each occasion, not to fit the occasion to precooked words. That requires a thoughtful effort. And as Samuel Johnson said long ago, "What is written without effort is in general read without pleasure."

Chapter 6

Tone: The Inner Music of Words

After you've squared away your lead, herded your paragraphs into place and swept up the small verbal debris, lend an ear. Does your copy sound conversational or stilted? Pompous or overly breezy? Formal or relaxed?

Tone ultimately determines whether your reader is pleased or not. Sentence structure has something to do with it, but tone is primarily generated by the choice of words. Plain, short, familiar words produce one distinct tone, fancy polysyllables another.

And then there are the "insides" of words. Many words have a special inner music—clusters of associations and images that lurk just below the surface.

House, home, residence and *domicile* all denote the same thing, but only a tone-deaf writer (which should be a contradiction in terms) would use them interchangeably, regardless of context. *The old couple lived in a cozy residence* rings false, but there's nothing wrong with *they changed their residence frequently.*

Emulate, copy and *mimic* refer to the same activity, but you wouldn't write that a worthy novice was *mimicking* a saint. You'd use *emulate,* because it has honorable connotations, while *copy* suggests a mindless, mechanical process, and *mimic* suggests an activity is being done in fun or with ridicule.

A word utterly misused destroys tone with a primal scream:

The executive finally *conceded* to his transfer.

Conceding is for defeat. In this case, you need more reporting to earn the word *conceded*. Does this transfer signify the executive had lost something through corporate intrigue? If you don't know that, you need a different word.

> But authorities said that the flight delays that wrenched thousands of travelers over the Thanksgiving weekend should ease ...

Not even the airlines can wrench you. Think *disrupted*, or simply, *affected*.

Most questions of tone are subtler. Consider these passages:

> But long-term positive aspects of the revolutionary process far transcended initial defects. The American Revolution was dynamic, not static, and took it upon itself to amend and improve imperfections in its structure.

> When George Bush's people took Sen. Sam Nunn aside at the end of 1988 and whispered in his ear that a job as defense secretary might be an offer, he told them not to bother. Mr. Nunn reckoned that, as chairman of the Senate Armed Services Committee, he already had as much say in matters of war and peace as he would get at the Pentagon. And after all, he said, he was a Democrat.

The first passage is from a newspaper, the second from a magazine. Both passages deal with serious subjects and both are clear, but they are octaves apart in tone. One is weighed down by ponderous abstract words of a distinctly academic flavor; you might say it's static, not dynamic. The other is almost conversational, skipping along on plain words and homely analogies. It calls to mind the frank talks that we imagine occurred in the smoke-filled backrooms of political lore. The tone reinforces the content of the paragraph.

AVOID SUDDEN SHIFTS

Tone need not be uniform, but sudden shifts are disconcerting, and a mixture of disparate tones grates like chalk on a slate.

Charles Dickens makes use of this effect with his immortal Mr. Micawber, whose passion for ornate language is happily tempered by his impulse to self-correction:

> Under the impression that your peregrinations in this Metropolis have not yet been extensive, and you might have difficulty in penetrating the arena of the modern Babylon ... *In short, that you might get lost ...*

Again and again Mr. Micawber, soaring, abruptly pulls himself back to earth. That's the side of him news writers should emulate.

Tone can go wrong in many ways besides turning pompous. It can, for example, become gushy, like the language you find in much advertising and promotion copy, in certain magazines and newspaper sections.

Words that usually signal gush are many, including *fabulous, tremendous, superb, unique, exquisite, gorgeous, fantastic, enchanting, incredible, glamorous* and the like. Public relations handouts are often gushers, and too much of that breathless verbiage slips through:

> Officials of the cable company said the long-awaited unveiling of the system will occur June 27, *ushering in a fabulous new viewing era* ...

The system will start operation June 27 says it all.

> The ship is *posh* from stem to stern, a floating *lap of luxury*, with *exquisite* food and a whirl of activities that keeps cruise passengers *tingling*.

It must be uncomfortable to float in a lap of luxury, exquisite or otherwise. No wonder the passengers tingle.

A gushy lead:

> There's something special about rivers, those winding and weaving waterways that just flow on and on. Lakes are lovely. Ponds are pleasant. But there's something about them—they just aren't rivers.

A New York critic starts a review this way:

> Excitement twinkled in the air like champagne bubbles in a spotlight ...

Which seems a good spot to stop reading.

WE ARE NOT AMUSED

Never treat death, pain and suffering—human or animal—lightly or humorously. The following story takes a persistently wrong tone:

So, you think you've got problems? Wait till you hear the story of Chuh-Chuh, the shih-tzu from Howard Beach.	Sour Note 1: The lead asks the reader to identify with a dog.

The dog's owners filed for $5.1 million damages yesterday in state Supreme Court, claiming they had suffered distress and psychological pain, while the dog suffered prolonged pain following castration by a veterinarian. ChuhChuh died in early August, nine days after the operation.

Sour Note 2: Details of animal's and owners' grief make flippant lead doubly dubious.

The veterinarian said the owner's attorney, Harry L. Lipsig, had a bark that is worse than his bite. Dr. Donald Wirth of the Lefferts Dog and Cat Hospital denied that he was responsible for the death of Chuh-Chuh.

Sour Note 3: More limp flippancy. Did the vet really say that?

"What the hell are they suing me for?" he said. "A lot of people have strong attachments to their pets. But this is outrageous. Shih-tzus are nice little dogs that cost about $300." Lipsig said, "There is the pain and suffering the poor creature went through. He was practically a member of the family."

Sour Note 4: "What the hell" quote is pointless.

It is part of the journalist's job to point out ridiculous things, but you must be sure others will share your view. Some readers might be amused by this treatment, but a great many more would put on a long face.

Few readers would chuckle over the lead to a story that police officers had "loads of trouble" recovering the body of a circus worker crushed by an elephant that fell on him.

Less flagrant but still using the wrong tone:

Mister Donut of America is suing a franchise holder for breach of contract, saying a police raid at the shop that uncovered crack cocaine and stolen property has left holes in the company's reputation.

I doubt that the company put it that way or that grins are in order here. For reasons of tone, likewise, don't refer to serious accidents as *mishaps*.

A man twisting his ankle stepping off a curb has a mishap; if a car hits him and he's paralyzed from the waist down, it's an accident. The word *incident* also suggests something of small consequence, a peripheral event—say, a picket line scuffle. A shootout in which several are hurt or killed is more than an incident.

BEWARE THE PERSONAL TOUCH

Addressing readers directly makes for a pleasantly personal tone in stories that lend themselves to this approach. But beware of casting readers in roles they can't readily envision for themselves, and don't link them to something disagreeable, as the lead of the dog story did.

If you've ever struggled with a garden full of weeds describes a situation ordinary enough that readers, nongardeners included, have no trouble seeing themselves in it. But when you write, *If you've ever thought about biting the head off a live chicken,* the personal note turns bizarre and the reader's response will be muted at best.

The following lead is lively and clever in that it mimics the writing style of the subject, a book author. But unless you are aware of that, it demands too much willingness to pretend:

> NEW YORK—You are practicing law in New York, supporting a family and paying the bills. But in your spare time, you are also writing children's books—in longhand, in your battered spiral notebook.
>
> What do you do? If you choose to remain a lawyer, this is the end of your story. But if you are Edward Packard, you chuck the law career ...

Somewhere soon in this list of particulars, the *you* is apt to stir uneasily and ask, *Who, me?*

DON'T BE ABSURD

The writer of the following passage is flirting with absurdity from the start and finally embraces it. The story concerns a sex education program for the very, very young. The exuberant tone adds to the difficulty of keeping a straight face:

> The child picked up the plastic model of a uterus, examined it closely and announced: "This looks like a frog."

The resemblance was remote, but his parents were nonetheless happy. They had begun a dialogue with their 3-year-old son that they hoped would continue through his childhood and adolescence.

The tone shuttles between the pompous and the cutesy and collapses with the unlikely suggestion of a serious dialogue with a 3-year-old.

Since the writer intended readers to take the project seriously, he would have done better to flatten out the passage, perhaps like this:

The child picked up the plastic uterus and said it looked like a frog. For the parents, it was the start of teaching their 3-year-old something about the facts of life. They want him to continue to discuss the subject with them freely through childhood and adolescence.

A far more subtle example is offered by a fine story that has perfect pitch except for two notes slightly off key. The writer is telling it through the youngsters' experiences, and the simple style is in tone and rhythm:

When 10-year-old Midaglia Roman learned that she wasn't promoted with her fourth grade class this year, she cried all the way home.

Today, Midaglia got her second chance. "I'd rather be here," the pretty, big-eyed girl said as she sat with about 30 others in a warm classroom at Public School 34, where the Board of Education is running a special summer school for students who were "left back" under a get-tough policy.

The story continues in this vein until:

Many, like Midaglia, will have a final try at the reading test when it's given again Aug. 14. They hope to *hone their skills* sufficiently in the coming week so they can go on with their class.

And, in a later paragraph:

But some students were less happy about the *intrusion on their summer plans.*

This story reads well as it stands. But the writer has been so attentive to keeping the tone modulated to youngsters' ways of thinking that the phrases *honed their skills* and *intrusion on their summer plans* add a sudden touch of stuffiness. *Brush up on their reading* and *missing out on some summer fun* might have been more consistent. Even kid slang would fit better.

DEALING WITH MOTIVE

Such nuances belong to the upper reaches of feature writing, perhaps. But dealing with motive is another matter, and can be a problem in straight news.

Motive sets the underlying basis for an individual's action—it matters in news stories. But we are not mind readers. And often, people may have mixed motives.

So motive needs delicate handling. That wasn't done in a story that had a governor, believed to be priming for a Senate race, "apparently courting the Jewish vote as he attacked the planned sale of $8.5 billion in arms to Saudi Arabia."

As AP President Lou Boccardi once commented in a note to the staff:

"*We* can't be so naive that we think governors speak without considering the political effects of what they say. But we also can't say the man is simply appealing for votes rather than expressing views truly held. It's clumsy and does him a disservice."

Better, but still wide of the mark:

> AUSTIN, Texas—Land Commissioner Bob Armstrong announced the "good news" today that the Permanent School fund had reached $3 billion, then admitted he was thinking about running for governor.

The writer doesn't say so outright, but the tone is unmistakable and the announcement is linked to political motive. Now, perhaps this journalist's reporting can point to a clear connection between announcement and ambition. But if not, it's important to keep these ideas separate.

It was done correctly in two stories where a news subject's special interests were mentioned as legitimate background without directly linking them to their statements. One concerned a speech by the sponsor of a bill to relax air pollution standards. He argued that the best way to clean up the air was to encourage people to junk their old cars and buy new ones.

Only after he had had his say, farther down in the story came a mention that the congressman represented a district where the auto industry was dominant.

Similarly, the fact that a congressman who spoke out against military base closings came from a district that would be directly affected was mentioned in the story—but not in the lead that dealt with his speech.

In both cases, the politicians may believe something is good policy even if they or their constituents stand to benefit. Whether or not that is the case, the journalist's job is to provide only the objective background, avoiding the nudge-and-wink approach of imputing motive without supporting facts. Motive is tricky.

NO HINTS, PLEASE

Matters of tone and motive loom large also in investigative stories where writers sometimes resort to hints and innuendoes and suggestive arrangements of damaging detail to establish what the evidence itself fails to demonstrate:

> *Incredibly*, Smith did not report his failure to file the returns until eight long years later.

> In another of those *remarkable "coincidences,"* the records were damaged by a *convenient* fire four days before the subpoena arrived. *Of course* the defendants claimed they hadn't known the records were being sought.

> The young prosecutor said *candidly* he had all but given up on the case. Doe, asked about the turn of events, withdrew once again into a *sullen* "no comment."

This tone is editorial, snide and, in essence, prosecutorial. And, paradoxically, it is usually much less effective than factual, detached statement. If you have solid information logically marshaled, the readers will draw their own inferences, without the aid of zingers.

They will be the more readily persuaded the less you resort to emotive words, small injections of opinion, knowing winks and lopsided selection of details. The less you comment or characterize, the better. An obvious attempt to push readers toward a foreshadowed conclusion is self-defeating; many resist such ham-handed pressure tactics. Research shows that once people understand you are trying to convince them of something, they trust you less.

Perhaps there's a mindset to investigative reporting that sometimes betrays writers into the prosecutorial tone. Gene Roberts, who retired in 1990 as executive editor of the *Philadelphia Inquirer*—which had a notable record of major investigative projects—touched on the subject in a discussion at an Associated Press Managing Editors convention.

"I think where many papers go astray in trying to do alleged investigative reporting is in defining it as unearthing criminals," he said. "This immediately casts the reporters as cops rather than as gatherers of information. Society will get along quite well without newsrooms that view themselves as police forces."

The journalists-as-cops analogy also limits what we can tell people about their world. The editor Michael Kinsley famously said that often "the scandal is what's legal." If journalists are only focused on law-breaking, they miss the opportunity to dig into the choices made by elected officials, corporations and others. Journalism is really about how communities define and identify problems in order to solve them. If our investigations are only about lawbreaking, throwing people in jail is the simple answer. If only societal problems were that simple.

WATCH IT, KIDDO

An informal, relaxed tone appeals to most people, but avoid excessive colloquialism and forced heartiness; don't get too chummy with your readers. It's an affectation and a form of writing down:

> The board of directors, after a daylong wrangle, lowered the boom on Smith. He was the third top honcho of the corporation to get the ax in as many years.

This is painful stuff, not because it offends the majesty of a corporation, but because backslapping breeziness has no place in a serious story.

A story retelling some of Iran's turbulent history also hits wrong keys:

> The late Shah, who *got kicked out* of the country in ...

> But he was forced into wandering when country after country *sent him packing.*

And similarly, an anniversary piece on the Russian revolution recalled that:

> In 1917, when the czar *got the boot ...*

A czar is forced from his throne, not booted or fired. Besides, this czar got more than the boot. The new Russian government killed him and his family.

Referring to news subjects by first name also carries informality too far. It's most often practiced on entertainment figures, athletes and other celebrities. The reporter is showing off a familiarity that's usually spurious, and the reader senses it.

It's different in writing about youngsters, when the use of the last name seems forced—up to age 15, anyway. Consistent use of the first name sounds more natural here. (However, if your lad has committed some ghastly, adult crimes, I would drop the first-name basis for obvious reasons.) And avoid references like *the Jones boy* or *the Smith woman*, which are simply rude.

EUPHEMISM: USE AND MISUSE

With all cultural indicators in our society pointing to the more explicit, "genteelism"—the refined tone that dotes on overly polite words and euphemisms—has been fading from daily journalism, though it still survives.

It survives in part because of jargon, which has invaded all parts of the language and, among other defacements, substitutes abstractions and euphemism for plain words: *disadvantaged* for *the poor, senior citizens* for *the elderly* or *old, interact* for *mingle with* or *make friends*, and many more.

Blather imported from the social sciences is a rich tributary to this variant of genteelism. Government is another fertile source. A fine example bowing in lately is *growing revenues*, much more agreeable than *tax increase*.

Other genteelisms, best avoided, are *mortician* for *undertaker, interment* for *burial, casket* for *coffin, lady* for *woman*, and *expecting* for *pregnant*. Even *pass away* for *die* still survives, and one Midwestern paper in a wedding story had the couple *motoring to their honeymoon haven*, a delightful archaism and most genteel.

All this is not to rule out euphemism entirely. We use it legitimately to avoid vulgarity or to soften something innately disgusting. Unlike genteelism, that is genuine politeness—to the reader. As Theodore Bernstein mildly put it in *The Careful Writer*, "It may be preferable to write that a man and a woman 'spent the night together' than to set forth in detail how they spent it."

Euphemism is objectionable only when used to doll up an emotionally stark but otherwise unexceptional fact of the human condition.

There's a directly musical aspect of tone that also deserves attention in news writing—those inadvertent collisions of syllables and sounds that cause readers pause (as *cause/pause* does in this sentence). A string of words ending in *tion*, for example, grates: *The organization gave attention to the situation. That fact doesn't detract from the act* is another disturbing sequence. A man innocently named Redding creates tiny havoc: *Redding, reading from his prepared text....* Such unlucky combinations, which are easily remedied, create a buzzing in the reader's head that distracts from the business at hand.

But you cannot force style and tone. If you do, you are courting disaster: Your prose turns a garish purple and sounds like a piano when the cat walks over the keys. All this writer was really trying to say is that Williams is shy and polite:

> Angry words launch themselves from deep inside Bernie Williams, his emotional silos opening and unleashing responses aimed at hurting an antagonist, the way Williams hurts when someone else fires slashing words at him. He never fires the first shot—his parents weaned him of this instinct long ago, reminding him that he needed to be respectful of others.

> Williams wants to retaliate, but before angry words escape his mouth, they lodge in his throat. They are choked off. He says ... nothing.

Words launch themselves, are fired when slashing, are unleashed by emotional silos, are choked off in the throat .... Some people may relish such overwriting as "colorful," but they are not among the knowledgeable.

One who was, the 18th-century lexicographer and critic Samuel Johnson, famously suggested that writers read over their stuff, and when they come across a passage "that you think is particularly fine, strike it out."

Tough love, sound advice to people given to fits and starts of "Fine Writing."

SIMPLICITY WILL DO

Tone, as we have seen, varies widely, depending on the story, the subject, the skill of writers, the passions of copy desks, and the preferences of editors. Tone is not the same at *The Wall Street Journal*, *The New York Times*, the *New York Post* and the *Los Angeles Times*. And newspaper tone certainly is not the same as what is found at online journalistic outfits that make up so much of the today's news production. News writing is often more personalized now. Where much old-school journalistic coaching works toward the goal of standardizing language and making the writer vanish into the background, today's journalists have license to use stylistic choices to distinguish themselves and develop unique voices that build connections with readers. That does change the tone of news writing, but not the mission.

There is not one universal tone to journalism, because telling readers what they need to know about the world around them can be done in many styles. What matters is that you write in a way that reflects reality and conveys meaning effectively. The plain style preferred here is rooted in journalism traditions. It speaks to readers without lecturing. It also demands that reporters have done the journalistic work. The even tone we counsel here avoids using attitude, or snark, to elide what the journalist has not done or to dress up assumptions and guesses as obvious facts.

Here's an example of the plain tone, taken from a story by AP Special Correspondent Jules Loh about the shooting of the town bully, the sort of story that often lures writers with a less disciplined ear into a rat-tat-tat, melodramatic style:

> He wasn't a street brawler. He was specific. He struck fear in your soul by staring you down, flashing a gun, occasionally using it. If you were his prey

for today he stalked you. He glared at you in silence and when he spoke it was in a slow whisper. Chilling.

He was born on a farm just outside of town. When he was a boy he fell off a hay wagon, requiring a steel plate to be implanted in his head. Some wondered if that was what made him so mean.

This is a small town: 440 people, filling station, bank, post office, tavern, blacktop street, grain elevator. Beyond lie rolling meadows, ripening corn, redwing blackbirds, fat cattle, windmills and silos, a scene off a Sweet Lassy feed calendar.

Ken McElroy jarred that pastoral serenity. So it is with outspoken relief that the citizens of Nodaway County now speak of him in the past tense. He is dead. The fear he brought them still lingers in a new, unexpected form …

Whatever gradations of tone you adopt, there can be no doubt about its importance for the writer. Barbara Tuchman, the historian, whose vivid prose combined with scholarship made her books best-sellers, said in an essay on her craft: "One learns to write by the practice thereof. After seven years' apprenticeship in journalism I have discovered that an essential element for good writing is a good ear. One must listen to the sound of one's own prose. This, I think, is one of the failures of much American writing. Too many writers do not listen to the sound of their own prose."

So listen.

Chapter 7

Pitfalls: Attributive Verbs and Loaded Words

SAID USUALLY SAYS IT BEST

Among attributive verbs, *said* usually says it best. It's short, clear, neutral and unfailingly accurate, a verb for all seasons.

You'll need substitutes occasionally to avoid monotony, but be careful; they are not true synonyms of *said*, not even—especially not—*stated* or *declared*.

Each attributive verb carries its own shade of meaning and must fit your context, a requirement remarkably often overlooked. *"Shut up," he explained*, is a fiction writer tongue in cheek. *"What, old Nobs!" ejaculated the son*, may have worked for Dickens, but sounds lewd to 21st-century readers. *"The sun rises every day," she recalled,* is a news writer foot in mouth.

Attributives kindle a craving for elegance in misguided souls, who reach for archaisms like *averred* or *asseverated*. One newspaper rolled its own attributive, with shaky results: *"The costs were rather higher than we anticipated," she assessed.*

You can still find some editors and writers who consider the repetition of an attributive verb within a 500-word radius a disgrace: Seen in print was a chaste initial *said* followed by *asserted, averred, proclaimed, avowed, propounded* and *opined*. The mounting suspense in following such a gaudy series was more gripping than the story.

SOME WIDELY MISUSED ATTRIBUTIVES

Let's consider the behavior of some widely used attributive verbs, listed in rough order of their usefulness:

> went on
> continued
> added
> insisted
> maintained
> complained
> cautioned
> explained
> recalled
> predicted

The first three words—*went on*, *continued* and *added*—are plain and as neutral as *said*. The others are simply descriptive; just make sure they fit the circumstances.

The following can be hazardous:

> pointed out
> noted
> warned
> charged
> claimed

To say that a speaker *points out* something invests it with an aura of fact. The reader mentally supplies "the fact that" after the verb. The point of a quotation is to introduce the source's subjective viewpoint; if it were factual information, you would paraphrase and attribute. This means that *point out* can have editorial nuances: *"The Democrats have seldom done this nation much good," the mayor pointed out* seems to subscribe to the mayor's verdict. When there's no such risk, confine *pointed out* to instances when a speaker calls attention to something that might otherwise be overlooked: *"The police weren't legally required to use a warrant in this case," the attorney general pointed out.*

Noted has similar connotations of fact and is even duller than *pointed out*.

Warned should be confined to quotes that point to genuine danger. Avoid lending credence to rhetorical overkill: *"A Republican victory will mean the end of civilization as we know it," the candidate warned.*

Charged is best left to legal contexts: *"The company has willfully broken the public trust,"* *the attorney general charged.* Don't use the word when casual criticism or mild complaints are involved: *"Some employees are stretching their coffee breaks to unconscionable lengths,"* *the director charged.*

Claimed is a far remove from the neutral *said.* For reason to be cautious, see the discussion of *claim* on page 73.

The following attributives are widely misused:

asserted
stated
declared
remarked
commented
observed
revealed

Asserted, stated and *declared* are often indiscriminately used for *said.* All are stronger and much more formal. To *assert* means to put forward an opinion or position strongly held. When that's done, the statement will speak for itself without benefit of that stiff *asserted. Stated* shouldn't be used at all; it is the instant mark of a wooden writer. (It fits if you're quoting from a deposition, but still looks dusty.) You *declare* a war, an emergency or martial law; the verb is too ponderous for most quotes.

Remarked applies to casual statements only: *"It's a fine day,"* *he remarked.* Not: *"Unless the Soviet Union withdraws from Afghanistan, our relations will continue on the present level,"* *the spokesman remarked.*

Commented also connotes the offhand or incidental, expressing a personal reaction or attitude: *"This is hardly his best work,"* *the principal commented.*

Observed is close in meaning to *remarked* and *commented,* but less conversational in tone and therefore less desirable.

God *reveals,* saints and mystics *reveal;* ordinary mortals *disclose.* Science may *reveal* a grand new cosmic concept, but a pediatrician *discloses* a new cure for colic.

Regrettably, all of the following keep cropping up in newsprint:

avowed
averred
opined
exclaimed
quipped
snapped

Avowed involves a strong moral commitment and is almost always overly dramatic. Its cousin, *vowed*, suggests a solemn oath, possibly sealed with blood from an index finger. *Promised* and *pledged* are invariably better.

Averred and *opined* should be relegated to Gothic novels or specialists in crossword puzzles.

Exclaimed usually underscores something that doesn't need underscoring.

Quipped is pointless when a real quip is quoted; too often, the writer applies it to a lame remark that lacks bite.

A person may *snap* one word, but hardly a sentence.

This last attributive verb brings us to applied physiology. Never use verbs denoting nonverbal processes as attributives, like *smiled, wept, laughed, chortled* or *growled*.

You don't smile words; you say them, smiling. *"I'm fond of him,"* she smiled, is no better than *"I'm very hot this morning,"* he radiated.

BEWARE LOADED WORDS

Some words can carry writers beyond what they intend to say and import value judgments into stories where they don't belong.

Reform is one such double-edged word. It means "to make better by removing faults or defects." That's why politicians, lawmakers and advocates attach "reform" to programs they're pushing.

But one group's reform is often another group's calamity. Tax changes labeled *reform* might leave half the electorate fuming. *Abortion law reform* may be welcomed as such by one side and abhorred by the other.

So, unless you're dealing with changes that the vast majority of reasonable citizens regard as beneficial (according to opinion polls, not your own subjective sense), you had better steer clear of calling them a reform on your own. Call them changes or proposals. If *reform* appears in the title of a bill or program that annoys as many as it pleases, make clear that *reform* is what the sponsors call it, not you.

Here are some other words to watch:

Admit, as in admitting a crime, implies yielding reluctantly under pressure. *The company chairman admitted that interest rates had not been factored into production estimates* suggests that he came clean after an astute reporter put the thumbscrews to him. In fact, he volunteered the information. Use *said* or *acknowledged*, unless the statement contradicts strongly asserted previous statements.

Bureaucrat. A slighting term for *official, civil servant* or *government employee*.

Candidly, frankly. The defense attorney said frankly that his case rested on a single witness. How do you know he was frank? Why not let statements speak for themselves, without such comments?

Claim is not a synonym for *say, assert* or *argue* unless you are writing in an academic context. You *claim* a (disputed) right. In a sentence like *the policeman claimed that he saw the gun,* the verb *claimed* casts doubt on his statement. If the question of what the policeman said is at issue in a legal proceeding, *claimed* works. If it is not a contested fact, the word introduces controversy where none exists. The word is used precisely in this sentence: *The company lawyers claimed that the patents extended to fast-film paper as well.* There's doubt, to be resolved in court. For the same reason, *"I'm a better singer than most of the younger performers," the diva claimed,* is sensible usage. But *"I've been in the Metropolitan Opera for 23 years," she claimed,* is silly if the statement is factual.

Loophole. Like *scheme* or *scheming,* the noun connotes sly, devious, perhaps unethical proceedings. That's not the case when taxpayers take advantage of such breaks as the tax laws afford. On the other hand, it's fair to write of a loophole when a lawyer discovers a way out of a contract due to an oversight that's plainly counter to the intent of the agreement.

Only. Even this worm can turn: *Only five of the nine administration measures got off the ground* suggests that the White House is fumbling.

Scheme. That's not another word for plan, just as *schemer* isn't the same as *planner. A scheme* suggests something shifty. That's not what the writer wanted to imply in, *American Airlines disclosed a scheme to lure new customers.*

Straightforward, steadfast. Characterizations that imply approval, just as *stubborn* implies disapproval. Some will consider the president's holding to his course as steadfast, others as stubborn.

Chapter 8

Quotes: Your Words or Mine?

News, to a remarkable degree, is what people say and how they say it—as actors in events, kibitzers, witnesses, social media commentators, informants, as movers and shakers and as the moved and the shaken. The chatter is incessant. So are the news writer's efforts to distill useful quotes from it.

Quotes, as even novices quickly realize, are indispensable. They lend authenticity. They put readers in touch with people as directly as print can manage it. Hearing the voices of those quoted helps make a story seem real, the people three-dimensional subjects.

But the quote has changed over the last 20 years. Multimedia presentations of news means the reader is also a viewer with full access to the comments made by a subject. And sources themselves (or their representatives) express themselves using new media. If anything, the chatter has gotten louder. The challenge for the reporter is to sift through the myriad possibilities to pick the quotations that will make a story.

Quotes are required, but they are not magic. When people don't scintillate, you won't get scintillating quotes. But you can be selective about what you use. Too many writers seem to assume that quotation marks, by themselves, can transform a grunt into a great fugue. *Smith said he accepted the job because it represented a "challenge."* Here they help not at all.

In leisurely interviews and other set pieces, skilled reporters can patiently cast their lines until a few gaudy fish rise to the bait. In the hot pursuit of ordinary news, there's much less opportunity for that. Quotes are often snatched on the run: a hasty comment from a harassed lawyer, a cop's police-blotter prose, the handful of dust stirred up by a bureaucrat scuttling for cover under a barrage of words. Increasingly, quotes are offered in new formats that require us to think deeply about authenticity.

Like other facts, quotes are not subject to revision. Once words are enclosed by quotation marks, they must be what the source said. Attempts to "improve" that by reshuffling or even changing words are high crimes and misdemeanors. The furthest you can go is to fix minor grammatical errors and omit pure padding or meaningless repetition. All you can do with the stuff, by way of direct quotes, is to take it or leave it. (But embracing the *leave it* can be liberating for the news writer.)

WHEN TO QUOTE?

Under these constraints, the art of handling quotes comes down to knowing when to quote, when to paraphrase and when to forget the whole thing. Sometimes the choice is simple. When a Navy secretary responds to reproaches that he's not sufficiently committed by saying, *"Lemmings are great team players, and see where they wind up,"* you quote him. When a preacher, threatened by Texas officials with shutting down a home for wayward girls, says, *"It may be the ninth inning and we may be behind in the score, but I see my bases loaded and Jesus Christ coming to bat,"* you'd hit that pitch out of the ballpark.

Most quotes aren't nearly so picturesque. When they sink below a certain level, a succinct paraphrase is the answer:

The senator said that "during this period of time, which covered six years, the subcommittee held a total of only six days of hearings."	The senator said the subcommittee held only six days of hearings in as many years.

The main distinction of the senatorial statement is 10 superfluous words. Some matter shouldn't be quoted at all:

> "I have presented to his excellency, President Hrawi, my letters of credence accrediting me as ambassador ... of the United States to Lebanon," Crocker told reporters after the 30-minute ceremony.

This is not electrifying; this the bureaucratic version of journalese. The following is sheer skullduggery:

> This suggests, the study said, that "although parents may be able to affect their children's cognitive skill acquisition, they may have relatively little influence on the ultimate level attained."

Occasionally, less-than-incisive remarks are worth direct quotation for the insight they give. A New York legislator, when asked about corruption in the state Assembly:

> "Personally speaking, for myself, to the best of my knowledge, I don't think I know anything, to the best of my knowledge."

The inability to formulate a clear answer contributes to our understanding of this legislator and his thinking about corruption. Good quotes should summarize what's on a person's mind, crystallize an emotion or attitude or offer an individual perspective of some sort—preferably in a concise and interesting way. They are subjective, rather than the authoritative narration the journalistic voice seeks to impart.

The following examples are both from *The New York Times*. In the first, a woman is quoted in an account of life in Nicaragua:

> "We can't make ends meet," said a 36-year-old waitress and mother of three who lives in the capital. "Everything's going up. We used to buy meat most days, but that's out of the question. We have to line up for hours for sugar and rice. And then we're told we can't have wage increases."

And this from a story about Northern Ireland's Maze prison, where IRA men were starving themselves to death:

> "By the time they get in here, there's no more belligerence, no more fight," said an attendant in the one-story, 10-bed hospital. "They're really quite cooperative and polite at this final stage. They just sit there and quietly die."

A paraphrase would have been sinful. But moreover, it would have been malpractice, journalistically. Capturing the sense of frustration or quiet resistance would not work from the reporters' perspective. The first-person style of the quotation makes the meaning more compelling.

What is said doesn't have to be remarkable in itself to carry a story forward. But note the difference the direct quotes make in this amusing intro:

> Yesterday was just one of those days for José Cruz. He got lectured by an 84-year-old grandmother, was surrounded by cops and arrested on two felonies after a seven-hour standoff.
>
> "I'm sorry, Ruth," said Cruz, 29, as police led him in handcuffs from the apartment of Ruth Wolko, whom he had held hostage in her fifth-floor apartment in Riverdale, Bronx.
>
> Earlier, Wolko told friends she had fed her captor a nice kosher breakfast and asked him, "Is this the only profession you have?"

When he answered, "Yes," she said, "Maybe you should go into some other profession." It began about 5 a.m. when Cruz allegedly was discovered looting a fourth-floor apartment.

When quotation marks, with their small subliminal drumroll, signal a human voice, the reader expects a pitch different from dryly factual recitation. Yet there is nothing but disappointment in the following story:

MIAMI—More than 6,300 exotic birds, from tiny finches to large parrots and macaws worth as much as $5,000 apiece, have been destroyed at an import center because of an outbreak of Newcastle disease, a virus that kills domestic poultry, federal officials said.

"All the birds here were destroyed and we are in the process of cleaning and disinfecting the area," said Connie Crunkelton, a spokeswoman for the U.S. Department of Agriculture.

Miss Crunkelton said federal officials feared that infected birds may have been shipped from Pet Farms Inc., the import company, within the past 30 days.

"We have notified the animal health officials in the states known to have received shipments," she said. "They will go to the facility and see if there are any infected birds. If so, they will have to be destroyed and the owners will be reimbursed for their loss."

There were 123 species and subspecies among the 6,300 birds destroyed at Pet Farms, Miss Crunkelton said. The owner will be reimbursed for the loss, she said.

"We don't have a dollar estimate on the birds as of yet, but we expect one later," Miss Crunkelton said.

Putting such pedestrian, fact-sheet information into direct quotation is like trying to set the telephone directory to music. Writers are usually better at stringing together words at the keyboard than sources are when thinking on their feet. A few words of paraphrase could have dispatched the details.

THE USES OF QUOTES

Besides adding living voices to the script, quotes perform certain standard functions. They are used to:

- Document and support third-person statements in the lead and elsewhere.

- Set off controversial material, where the precise wording can be an issue, as in legal contexts.

- Catch distinctions and nuances in important passages or speeches and convey some of the flavor of the speaker's language.

- Highlight exchanges and testimony in trials, hearings, meetings and other garrulous encounters.

Quotes should pull lustily on the oars to help move the story along, as in this example:

> SAN SALVADOR (AP)—Terrorists fired three anti-tank rocket grenades at the United States Embassy today, causing some damage but apparently no injuries, security forces reported.
>
> They said the grenades were probably fired from a building about 60 yards away from the embassy compound.
>
> "Something put a hole in one of our upper stories, but as far as we can tell nobody was hurt," said an embassy spokesman reached by telephone.
>
> Another embassy employee said the damage was on the third floor, which houses the office of Ambassador Robert E. White, but the ambassador was not in the embassy at the time.

The third graf backs up the lead and adds a bit of fresh detail. Repetition is the great danger. Even robust quotes turn sickly as a reprise of something that's just been reported in third person:

> The chairman announced that the company would start the most ambitious engineering project in its history.
>
> "We'll launch our most ambitious engineering project ever," he told applauding stockholders.

PERTINENCE MAY DECIDE

Newsworthy speeches, whether scintillating or not, require considerable direct quotation. After all, the news in a speech story is the way the speaker framed and presented an issue or idea. Here pertinence overrides color: It's advisable to give significant passages in the speaker's own words even if they are fairly tedious.

This was not a problem in the following example, a happy meeting between a strong expressive text and a writer, John Edlin, who knew how to make the most of it from cutting the partial quote of the lead to the extended quotation in the last paragraph:

SALISBURY, Zimbabwe (AP)—Prime Minister Robert Mugabe said Thursday the black states of southern Africa must free themselves from foreign economic exploitation that has made them either "puppets or perpetual beggars."

Mugabe, opening the ministerial session of the Southern African Development Coordination Conference at a Salisbury hotel, accused unscrupulous foreign investors of maintaining a relentless grip on southern Africa's resources.

"We remain dominated economically by economic lords as we were politically dominated by political lords yesterday," said the prime minister of newly independent Zimbabwe, the former British colony of Rhodesia. "Economic domination is indeed a worse phenomenon than political domination."

Mugabe said, "Our resources are wasting away day by day as they get freighted to Paris, London and New York."

He said the nine nations taking part in the conference on "economic liberation" have recognized that they are "fragmented, grossly exploited and subject to economic manipulation by outsiders."

The prime minister particularly criticized multinational corporations which he said arrange a "mouse's share for us and a lion's share for themselves." Black African nations, he said, are imprisoned by unfavorable trading conditions. They sell their raw material cheaply but have to pay "exorbitant" prices for imports.

"Thus we meet foul play in both cases," he said. "And whether we play at home or away, ours is perpetual defeat, theirs perpetual victory. Is it any wonder that we have been turned into either economic puppets or perpetual beggars?"

The reader has enough in Mugabe's own words to judge both the substance and tone of his argument and catch a glint of his personality as well.

But we must be careful in this regard. Quoting may introduce the subjective viewpoints of sources into our stories, but the presence of quotation marks does not absolve us from our journalistic commitment to truth. What use is clear writing if we render falsehoods in more effective ways?

We must make judgments about when a quotation is offered as good faith analysis and when it is being used strategically to obscure the truth. We are not mind readers, which means we often may be checking statements against past pronouncements. When in doubt about the veracity of a claim, paraphrase and attribute rather than quoting directly. When your story is about the false claim, point out the claim is false before repeating or paraphrasing it.

HELP WANTED (SOMETIMES)

Quotes sometimes need a little internal stitching. A parenthetic insert may be used to explain a technical word or to clarify a pronoun reference: *"He said he had no idea why he (Smith) didn't show up for work with the others."* But a little stage-whispering goes a long way. It's drowning out the quote here:

> "I guess he (the driver) just hates hitchhikers. They (highway motorists) do it all the time. They swerve at you like they're trying to hit you. This is the first time one of us (referring to highway tramps in general) ever really got hit."

When a quote needs that much help, you're better off paraphrasing.

The ellipsis (...) indicates omitted matter. The trouble is that it calls attention to what is not there rather than to what is. It's sometimes necessary, for example in quoting government reports or legal documents, when sentences are excerpted from a coherent larger passage. But an ellipsis is seldom required in the ordinary run of conversational and interview quotes, which readers know to be excerpts anyway.

Clues and identification enabling readers to understand a quote normally should precede rather than follow it; the cryptic quote at the start of a paragraph is an annoyance.

> That optimism assumed that passengers would return fairly quickly, airline executives say. But doubts about safety, along with a soft economy, have kept large numbers of passengers away, producing grim near-term prospects for several carriers.
>
> "I don't agree with that," said an airline official about the view that the carriers would profit from the slowdown.

The reader is momentarily misled into believing that the disagreement refers to the grim near-term prospects.

THE *SAID OF* TRAP

Writers sometimes plunge into the *said of* mode to clarify something that's already clear from the context:

While the players did not know that Michael was on the verge of being dismissed yesterday, they knew his job had been on the line at least once this season and, based on their experience, they knew that the team's principal owner often pressures and embarrasses his employees in a belief that it will improve their performance.

"That may work in one facet of life but not in this one," Watson *said of* Steinbrenner's techniques.

"Stick will be here," George Steinbrenner *said of* him that day last November.

Another example:

"It's rare. We don't usually get that many large petitions," Richard Markse, a railroad spokesman, *said of* the 300 signatures Fields collected.

More clearly put:

Fields collected 300 signatures. "It's rare," said Richard Markse, a railroad spokesman. "We don't usually get that many large petitions."

From a story about a dowser's trade:

"*I* feel a little tingle and it starts moving," Austin *said of* his divining rod.

Clueing the reader in more effectively:

Describing the workings of his divining rod, Austin said, "*I* feel a little tingle and it starts moving."

HAPHAZARD ATTRIBUTION

Make sure the reader always knows who's speaking, but don't overattribute in running quotations:

"I call that dead water. I can't find dead water in underground caverns." Austin calls moving water "live water" and says that is the only water he can find. "It's got to have some movement to it," *the dowser said.*

Don't drop attribution haphazardly into a quote where it will disrupt the flow of a sentence:

"The charge is not," the lawyer said, "warranted in the slightest degree."

"This is the second time," the angry senator said, "the agency has violated its own regulations."

Put the sinuous lawyer and the angry senator at the start or at the end of their sentences. When attribution goes within a sentence, it should fit smoothly between clauses or where a speaker might naturally pause:

> "I thought I'd be free long before then," she said, "but it hasn't worked out that way."

FRAGMENTARY QUOTES

An indiscriminate rage to quote, or perhaps a sense of insecurity, traps writers into pointless fragmentary quotes, consisting of one or two unremarkable words used in their ordinary sense:

> The mayor said a "key" element of his plan was the parking complex. He noted it had the support of "many citizens."
>
> The critic called it a "wonderful" movie.

Had our critic called it "incandescent," however, quotation marks would be proper. The word is sufficiently unusual to rate the epaulets.

The quotation marks also are justified in cases like the following:

> When arrested, Smith said he was an "importer." (*To convey doubt.*)
>
> The president said Reagan was in no sense a "racist." (*To make clear that the president himself used this highly charged word.*)
>
> The Soviet news agency Tass said today that "criminal activities" had occurred in Kabul. (*In the West, it was called something else.*)

WATCH THE CONTEXT

Next to getting the actual words right, the most important thing is to keep quotes in context. Failure usually arises from careless compression that makes a statement appear more emphatic than it is. A qualification may be dropped or buried, a speaker's elaboration of a point overlooked or a remark intended as jocular reported deadpan.

It may be tiresome when a newsmaker surrounds his assertions with *ifs*, *buts* and *maybes*, but if he elects to crawl, the writer must not force him into a trot.

Special caution is indicated with the use of partial quotes in leads. Qualifications should either stay within the quote or follow immediately. Even if the full quote, with its amplified or softened meaning, appears later in the story, it's not enough; the reader may not get that far.

Consider the full statement on the left and the new version on the right:

"There may be occasions, crimes, when the death penalty appears justified. At least many people think so. I have sometimes leaned that way myself, but to my mind, large problems always remain." A longtime opponent of capital punishment said today that on occasions "the death penalty appears justified."	"I have sometimes leaned that way myself," he added, though "large problems always remain."

The partial quotes are accurate, but the meaning—the tentative tone—has been subtly altered.

Not so subtle is what befell James Watt, secretary of the interior under Reagan, who found himself sandbagged with a striking sentence that was widely quoted without the rest of the passage.

At a congressional hearing, Watt was asked if he believed that some resources should be conserved for future generations. His full reply:

> "Absolutely. That is the delicate balance the secretary of the interior must have to be steward for the natural resources for this generation as well as future generations. *I do not know how many future generations we can count on before the Lord returns.* Whatever it is, we have to manage with skill to have the resources for future generations."

Perhaps an official sophisticated about the ways of the media should have scented peril in injecting religious musings into his testimony, but those who seized on the italicized sentence in isolation certainly conveyed a meaning different from that of the complete passage. It's something the conscientious news writer will guard against.

You can also skew a quote by converting a long, involved question into the subject's answer:

> Reporter: Do you feel the verdict was wrong, that it was a gross miscarriage of justice? A: *Well, yes.*

> Copy: *He said he "felt that the verdict was wrong and a gross miscarriage of justice."*

Did he? Reporters shouldn't ask double-barreled questions, which combine two queries into one, because you're never sure what part the interviewee is responding to. You deal with it by clearly differentiating: He said "yes" to a reporter's question whether he felt, etc.

In the following passage, the practice is carried to absurdity:

> Eighty-seven percent of those surveyed in the national poll said they "feel personally, deeply involved with the fate of the hostages and are willing to wait as long as necessary to get the hostages back unharmed."

Must have been an interesting chorus. The quote, of course, refers to the survey question.

Never attribute a direct quote to more than one person, unless you've stumbled on a group that speaks in perfect unison. The following appeared in a newspaper:

> Feminists hurled abuse as the men competed in a Bavarian park to become the fastest tree planter. "*We* don't accept the perpetuation of the masculine image," they yelled.

The New Yorker ran the item under the heading, "Yells We Doubt Ever Got Yelled."

OVEREXTENDED ATTRIBUTION

Although indirect quotation offers more latitude, there are similar traps. Be sure not to attribute to the source wording and coloring obviously different from the source's own:

> WASHINGTON—The nation's unemployment rate shot up from 6.2 percent to 7 percent in April, the highest level in $2\frac{1}{2}$ years *and a powerful sign that the inflation-wracked economy is now being squeezed by the rise of recession,* the government reported today.

All very true, no doubt, but that's not how the government's report put it. In the following instance, the attribution is just overextended:

> "It affects your whole life," said Wilson's pretty wife, Nancy, whose job as a court clerk helps to sustain them. "You're on edge. It's like a disease you're waiting to catch."
>
> The disease has reached epidemic proportions in the black community, which suffers from a jobless rate of 30 percent, says the Rev. Thomas Robinson, head of the Opportunity Industrialization Center.

The Rev. Mr. Robinson, however, didn't say anything about diseases and epidemics.

A period after *community* and a new sentence would keep things straight.

A BAND-AID MAY HELP

We have stressed that direct quotes must faithfully reproduce what the speaker has said. There are times, however, when in an interview, minor grammatical slips could be corrected; hardly anyone is free of such mistakes in casual speech. The purpose is not to make anyone look good, but to make things easier for the reader.

For example, a story quoted Secretary of the Treasury Regan as saying: "Jim Baker knows more about politics than I'll ever know. But I think I know more about finances than *him*." The writer could safely have made that *he*, or, better yet, stopped the quote at *finances*.

Note that we are talking about mini adjustments. Heroic intervention to straighten out gaping incoherencies is another matter. When a politican, say, replies to a question in a way that betrays monumental trouble in coming to grips with it, don't tighten and smooth quotes into a masterpiece of concise statement. Judgment, fairness and even-handedness are the guides to navigating these shoals.

What about people who speak generally poor English, street language, use *ain't* and *that there's*? How far you go in using offbeat idiom depends on the purpose of the story. If it's to portray life in a remote corner of the country, snippets of nonstandard English, peculiar phrasing and the occasional double negative will add depth and flavor without offense.

But in most news stories, such speechways are simply irrelevant. You might call attention to a man's limp if he's just entered a track meet, but not if he's walking to the subway.

To illustrate from a story about a tavern shooting in Oregon:

> No motive for the shooting was established.

> "He didn't say nothing," said Brent Yagle, a patron of the popular nightspot frequented by people mostly in their 20s. "He just opened the door and started firing. I didn't think the shots were real until I saw people drop."

> The tavern owner, John Helton, said, "I do hope he had some kind of reason and didn't do it just 'cause he was in the mood."

The double negative and bobtailed *because* merely contribute a whiff of condescension. Better to paraphrase the first: *The man said nothing, according to Brent Yagle....* And spelling out *because* would have violated no higher truth.

The following underscores the distinctions involved in this minor house-breaking. An AP story plumbed the mood of Asheville, N.C., in an election year. The intro centers on a series of quotes:

> "Half this country keeps the other half going," says a bitter housewife in line at the checkout counter. Ahead of her is a man buying more meat than she can afford. He pays with food stamps.

> "We can't do anything about those crazy Iranians holding our people," writes a rural editorialist, "but we can do something about taxes. We can control them."

> "I'm relatively affluent, but will I be able to send my kids to college?" asks the executive director of what used to be a pillar of American optimism, the local Chamber of Commerce.

> "The election?" ponders an old mountaineer. "I ain't heard it mentioned except on the TV."

The last quotee appears in the character of a mountaineer, an archetype, you might say, and the *ain't* is as natural as the plug of tobacco in a pitcher's cheek. No need to paraphrase.

EXPLETIVE DELETED

Profanity, vulgarity and obscenity present another kind of problem. Society has become vastly more permissive toward them in most forms of print, films and theater. Newspapers increasingly struggle to account for coarse language in the corridors of power. The challenge is representing the news accurately without letting specific words derail a story over questions of taste, which is by nature subjective. The limits of the acceptable vary from outlet to outlet.

It's good advice—and AP policy—to avoid casual profanity and vulgarisms. Many swear words and expletives are so routine at certain levels of conversation in many groups that they're like other verbal fillers that can simply be dropped from a direct quote. When that seems awkward, paraphrase.

The practical test on admitting expletives is whether they are essential to the story. They seldom are. A celebrated exception 1979 was Jimmy Carter's unpresidential language referring to Sen. Edward Kennedy in promising to "whip his ass." Even so, some papers fig-leafed the noun with dashes or asterisks.

Since Carter's day, reticence toward "ass-kicking" in high places has diminished. George Bush has been quoted to that effect at least twice, first as vice president and then as president.

The mild profanity in the following example is also indispensable in giving the earthy flavor of a tough lady who had kept federal inspectors off her coal mine at gunpoint:

> When her cousin tried to fetch her she leveled a pistol at him and told him to get lost. A masher got fresh once while she was waiting tables and she scalded him with coffee. Her refusal of favors to another man included smashing his windshield with a tire iron. Don't cross Violet Smith.

> "Hell, kid, them feds have never scared me.

> "One time when I was running a little grocery in Durango, an Internal Revenue agent came in and said I haven't paid my taxes. I had. I flattened the S.O.B. with my fist and kicked his rear end out of the door."

Violet Smith, incidentally, does not abbreviate S.O.B.

Ultimately the question is not about the specific words, but whether you can tell the story more effectively using different ones. The point of news writing is to transmit information. If four-letter words detract from that in some way, it's best to find ways around them.

PARAPHRASE TO THE RESCUE

A few final points on quotes:

- We're not in the business of protecting people from their own flapping tongues, but it's poor practice to make somebody look foolish in print when he has innocently misspoken himself:

> "What is lacking is not indifference and apathy," suggests Joseph Guinn, vice president of the association. "The general public just doesn't understand the educational value."

> He meant that apathy and indifference were not the problem, and both he and the reader should have been rescued by paraphrase.

- Here you have the right way and the wrong way of using fragmentary quotes in one sentence:

ATLANTA—A police officer testified today that he stopped Wayne B. Williams near a Chattahoochee River bridge because a "loud splash" made the officer "pretty suspicious."

The first phrase doesn't rate the quotation marks; the second does, as the precise description of the officer's feelings.

- The more that quotes resemble dialogue in form, the livelier they are. An exchange gives readers a special sense of participation. Here is an example from a routine news conference:

Dick Moe, an aide to the vice president, told reporters: "I think both sides are in a position to go to the other and, depending on who prevails, seek their support in the general election."

"And get it?" he was asked.

"And get it."

- In some stories, usually features, it's possible to trim superstructure for a similarly crisp effect. Compare the elaborate setups on the left with the version on the right:

When asked if she admired her mother's cooking, Miss Johnson replied, "It was fabulous." In response to a query about her own cooking skill, she conceded it was "not so hot."	What of her mother's cooking? "Fabulous." Her own? "Not so hot."

- Partial quotes should fit into the grammatical structure of the sentence.

The chairman emphasized that he "insists on equal pay for equal work."

Did he say, "*I insists*"? No. So move the opening quotation mark or paraphrase.

- Avoid double attribution.

The commissioner said he would move promptly against what he called "an outrageous situation."

Use either *what he called* or the quotation marks, but not both.

- As in a primitive ritual, certain quotes recur automatically in similar news situations. People have many times read or heard those phrases and will mouth them when opportunity offers. By now these quotes have the appeal of bovine cud. But unless someone breaks the chain, they will continue until they become the last syllables of recorded time. Here are a few such prefabricated phrases that ought to be passed by:

"It's a great challenge." Starlet about her new role, executive about his new job, coach on taking over a team of ragged bums.

"I like people," in various nauseating configurations. Worth quoting if a mass murderer says it.

"It sounded like 10 (15, 100) freight trains." Applicable to all tornadoes.

"It sounded like an atom bomb going off." Any explosion. If the speaker actually heard an atom bomb going off, write about him.

Chapter 9

Color: Dip Your Brush in Small Details

Elsewhere in this book, we discuss how reporters need to develop a good ear to fit words together gracefully. To fit words together colorfully, they need to develop a good eye.

Color implies a way of *seeing* a story so you can show the reader. Adjectives and intensifiers have nothing to do with it—they are, in fact, great deceivers.

Why inform readers that something is dramatic or tragic? Give them the particulars, and they will supply their own adjectives.

What real image do you call up by describing a resort as *posh* or a military reservation as *sprawling*? What's distinctive about the *white, sandy* beach? Most beaches are. Or about the city that *is a city of many contrasts*? The same can be written about every city, and probably has been.

Color is a matter of the right details—observed directly, elicited from witnesses, always with the breath of actuality. It works even in a report as routine as one on a city council hearing:

> As the hearing droned on past midnight, half the audience had left. But the woman in the front row was still knitting away at her red sweater. In back, a middle-aged man, head down, was snoring gently. Councilman Smithers seemed to be counting the patches of peeling plaster on the walls, while Saunders rested his chin on the gavel. There was no further need of pounding.

Tiny details and a splash of real color in an unlikely setting. How many reporters would have gone to the trouble?

Here's a passage from a column by the late Red Smith, describing a morning at the racetrack:

> Through the fragrance of the wood fires burning under the elms in the stable area behind Saratoga's main track, wreaths of morning mist curled up to be burned away by slanting rays of sunshine. Hot-walkers led horses in lazy circles behind the barns, while other horses stood relishing the flow of cold water from garden hoses trained on their forelegs.
>
> Grooms swathed horses with soapy sponges and rubbed them dry. The rhythmic throbbing of hooves could be heard from the track itself, where the horses were working.

And here's an AP story, in an entirely different vein. Again, the scene is set with strong particulars:

> Like a candy bar in the hands of a 2-year-old, crude oil from the *Exxon Valdez* has gotten into everything.
>
> Globs of mousse litter the cobbled beach. Rainwater beads up on rocks as on the waxed hood of a car. A cleanup worker digs into the sand and his hand comes up a greasy brown.
>
> A burly fisherman breaks into tears as he describes steering his boat through the slick: no water lapping, no birds crying, just the sickening silence of oil slipping past the hull.
>
> At a bird rescue center in Seward, some of the patients are failing. They have been washed clean, but not before swallowing fatal doses of oil. They don't cry out; instinct tells them not to advertise their distress to predators. "They just get real quiet, sit in a corner and die," says rescue coordinator Jay Holcomb.

SMALL, SPECIFIC DETAILS

For color, reporters cannot rely on phrases and fancy—or ready-made—figures of speech. They rely on hard particulars. They must train themselves to spot those small, specific details that give intimate glimpses into the nature of their subject. This is how journalists show, rather than tell.

Jules Loh, in a profile of Herbert Hoover, noticed that among many items on the former president's desk was a tumbler containing a dozen well-sharpened pencils—a detail that most good reporters would pick up. But he also noticed that the erasers on the pencils were worn down. That detail told more about the man than all the obvious ones: the color of his necktie, the shine on his shoes, the handkerchief in his breast pocket.

When Pulitzer Prize laureate Saul Pett wrote a story on the workings of the mind of Robert McNamara, he never used the words *mind like a computer*. He didn't have to. He conveyed this idea by attention to detail during a dinner interview, describing McNamara as:

> ... judiciously weighing the options of having a second drink or not, evaluating all the factors in selecting between fish or beef and, once having made up his mind, never looking back.

Here's the start of a story on the slow death of small towns in the Great Plains. The piece can be done, and often has been done, in abstractions, demographics, trends, statistics—the Big Picture approach (which tends to be dull). Stories like this need to grounded in data, of course, but a town's decline is also something experienced.

AP reporter Sharon Cohen opens with a close-up of one elderly man, then builds her narrative with vivid, precise details. What emerges visually is not unlike the camera work of a gifted film producer.

> SHEYENNE, N.D. (AP)— It's Sunday morning and Norris Rud is singing hymns in the tiny white clapboard church he has prayed at since the days of lantern light. His pew offers a view of flat, frozen, endless prairie. But his eyes see something else:
>
> Family history.
>
> It was a mile down the winding gravel road, past the shuttered, rotting one-room schoolhouse, where his grandfather Nels planted the first trees more than 100 years ago, staking claim to a chunk of America's frontier.
>
> It was at the same altar where Rud takes communion that he was baptized one morning 73 years ago.
>
> And it's just outside the frost-covered stained glass windows where his kin— Ruds and Hendricksons, Norwegian emigrés who journeyed by ship, then by rail to this windswept land—now lie buried among clunky weathered gray headstones.
>
> The small cemetery at Grandfield Lutheran Church is growing.
>
> Most everything else around here is not.

An intelligent choice of small details brings far more vitality to a story than mere statement (the old "show, don't tell" doctrine).

Some writers might ask why anyone would lavish a whole paragraph on this summarizing sentence:

The Taiwanese these days are showing much more interest in their own culture than before.

The Wall Street Journal wisely chose to lavish, with this graf:

> Restaurants with 1940s decors and playing Taiwanese oldies are packing in the customers by serving pricey dishes that grandma used to make. Books on Taiwanese culture and history are flying off the shelves. Troupes performing Peking opera, the national art form of China, have had grant money cut, to be spent instead on Taiwanese puppet masters versed in local folklore.

Now you see, as well as understand.

Sometimes it's difficult or inconvenient to plod after details, but that's where Joe Smith, the writer, relies on Joe Smith, the reporter. AP Newsfeatures writer Sid Moody discussed this in a postscript to a story he wrote about an ocean crossing on a square-rigged Norwegian sailing ship:

> You're looking for detail, verbs of description instead of adjectives or adverbs. Sure, the helmsman stands at the wheel like a Viking. But he also clamps his lips into a line to keep out the rain, narrows his eyes to gunslits against the wind, stares transfixed as a swami at the compass light. His knuckles are white from the cold and the strain of the helm. He sails on. The reader may have his own idea of what a Viking is, but you're out there in the wet to tell him what this particular Viking did on this particular ship in this particular storm, and if you can't give him specifics, you might as well go below and be warm and dry and eat goat yogurt.

PSEUDO-COLOR WON'T WORK

No, grand generalizations and indistinct noun-adjective combinations don't add color to writing; particulars do. Here's an example of pseudo-color from a news story about a newly appointed immigration commissioner:

> Outside the state capitol he is said to be essentially mild-mannered. With his modishly styled hair, neat mustache and hornrimmed glasses, he could be taken for a professor from the nearby University of Texas.

On the basis of that description, so could half the male population. And note the ponderous qualifier before that daring characterization, *mild-mannered*. George Clooney is mild-mannered, and so was Willie Sutton, the bank robber. Finally, what does a college professor look like? There are college professors who could be taken for plumbers, undertakers, corporation chairmen, engineers and homeless people. These descriptions are not about the subject, they are about the writer's world view and social categories.

This kind of mush just amounts to a string of words, adding up to a clichéd portrayal that you've read before in a thousand inconsequential contexts.

Contrast this terse sentence in an AP story describing a craftsman who reproduces Shaker furniture:

> Charles Caffal is a 43-year-old artisan, built along the lines he admires most. He is as lean as a clothespin—a Shaker invention—and his only ornamentation is a full, reddish beard.

This is a rich image in a few words, and a long way from the essentially mild-mannered, bespectacled gent who could be taken for your typical college professor.

Not every story is suitable to color. A presidential announcement, a report on rising interest rates, various government actions—not much chance for visual writing there.

In fact, details squirted on austere facades where they don't belong merely irritate, like graffiti.

Any story about the politician Dennis Kucinich invariably referred to his height, which had nothing to do with anything he was saying.

Somewhere in almost every story on Adm. Poindexter testifying at the Iran-Contra hearings, the adjective "pipe-puffing" surfaced, without ever achieving relevance.

A story on a woman desperately telephoning police for help notes—in the lead, no less—that her phone was "cream-colored." What's the difference?

In stories on court procedures, writers seem to feel compelled to describe the principals' clothes. That's OK if the prosecutor wears a leotard, but:

> Miller, wearing a tan suit over his large frame, took notes while Schiff delivered his opening statement. Miller's two sons, wearing gray business suits, were among the spectators.

> List, wearing a light-brown suit and tie, sat stone-faced ...

> As Moore, wearing a long-sleeved shirt and tie, walked to the prison building ...

DON'T OVERDO IT

Flatness is a greater problem in news writing than excessive color, but color can be overdone.

A scuffle between two drunks, however picturesque, at a political gathering doesn't rate a burst of description high in a report of a presidential candidate's campaign speech. Like so much else in this intricate business, color requires a sense of balance and proportion, impossible to define, and every colorful detail must pass the test of relevance.

When you're trying too hard, this is what can happen:

> HOUSTON—Leaders of the seven richest nations convened today for a summit that could reshape the world's economic landscape to nourish the dizzying blossom of East-West peace and stem a tenacious underbrush of trade and environmental disputes among themselves.

Part of writing is knowing when the colorful details do not fit. It is hard to walk away from something that you alone have observed. This is why in countless celebrity interviews we're told that the subject dispensed her wisdom over a spinach salad in a trendy upscale Los Angeles restaurant. Honestly, mention the menu if it's filleted rattlesnake or if the meal choice relates to a theme of the story. Otherwise you're just bragging about having had lunch with a famous person.

WHEN COLOR WORKS

Let us conclude the dissertation on color with two examples where, integral to each story, color works exactly right.

The first is from a story that dealt with a controversy about convict road crews. After outlining the issues and describing the work, writer Andrew Petkofsky of the *Richmond News Leader* took his readers to the scene:

> The crew had started at the Henrico County line about a month before and worked steadily through some of the summer's hottest days.

> This day was cool and lovely, however, and the prisoners in blue work clothes and orange hard hats had plenty of time to gripe to a reporter as they hefted shovels, rakes and brooms. The uniformed young man standing guard with a 12-gauge shotgun listened impassively. He had heard it all before.

Note the precision of visual detail.

Second, consider this vivid lead about an accordion store run by millennials from the *Philadelphia Inquirer*; every detail has a purpose setting the scene in a story about a shop that does not conform to expectations.

> New accordions in the Liberty Bellows showroom are stacked and arranged like jeweled beetles at a natural-history museum, some with shells as green as

a lime's rind and others with keys like red velvet cake. Some are adorned with ruby-colored rhinestones, to catch the eyes of the Mexican norteña players, and others have a simple, dark sheen like coffee direct from Italy.

There are accordions in boxes in every crevice and alcove in the narrow Queen Village shop, a former Second Street salon just off South.

Someone was playing an accordion beneath a stuffed bobcat on the second floor, and there were more accordions shelved in bits and pieces another floor up, never to be played again. There were even pictures of scantily clad women holding accordions in the men's room.

One thing Liberty Bellows doesn't have is what you might expect when you think of accordions: an Old World master, hunched over beneath a lamp with sawdust in his hair, wearing a shellac-stained apron and magnifying glasses to make all of an accordion's tiny innards look larger.

Instead, there's Dorie Byrne. She's 33 and plays in a trio of bands. On Friday, just before lunch, she was fixing an accordion strap wearing a vintage mechanic's shirt, bandanna, and chemistry lab goggles. She had a Rosie the Riveter look, and it fit. "I'm just riveting this stupid thing," Byrne said, tapping a little hammer on a leather strap.

Color is a way of seeing a story. On behalf of reporters who prefer to operate on sonar, like bats, we can only intone the Old Testament verse: "Lord, I pray thee open his eyes that he may see."

Chapter 10

Pseudo-Color: Clichés and Other Trespasses

We now pass from living color into the nether world of clichés, misshapen figures of speech and strained comparisons. These, too, spring from the laudable impulse to brighten copy, but the tools are shoddy and so are the results.

Clichés by definition are threadbare phrases that good writers try to avoid. George Orwell, a purist in style, advised long ago: "Never use a metaphor, a simile, or a figure of speech that you are used to seeing in print."

The general idea is sound, but the prohibition too sweeping. No writer can do entirely without the large stock of familiar expressions that includes hardworking idiom, phrases somewhere between idiom and cliché (*off base*, *snowed under*) and cliché unalloyed.

The late Eric Partridge, who heroically compiled a *Dictionary of Clichés*, conceded that what constitutes a cliché is partly a matter of opinion. Set a brace of editors to hunting down clichés in the same story and some of their trophies will be different; one may gag at a phrase that doesn't ruffle the other.

The way in which you use a tired expression also bears on its cliché status. Sir Ernest Gowers, another accomplished word man, says it depends on whether clichés "are used unthinkingly as reach-me-downs or chosen as the best means of saying what a writer has to say."

Furthermore, not all clichés are obnoxious to the same degree. Some are so abysmal that no self-respecting writer will touch them in any context: *Selling like hotcakes, breath of fresh air, last but not least, shun like the plague and leave no stone unturned* are among the pariahs. (A selected list of other mangy expressions appears at the end of this chapter.)

But in many cases, no summary beheading is necessary. *Sour grapes* or *white elephant* are greatly worn, but each can summarize something specific in a useful way.

CLICHÉS AT ARM'S LENGTH

Here are a few suggestions on dealing with clichés—at proper arm's length (cliché? idiom?) but without hysteria:

- Don't worry about an occasional cliché, but start stringing a few together and your story wilts. With each additional cliché in a passage, the staleness increases exponentially. That's what happened in the following political story:

  1st graf: They're *throwing out the rule book* in Nassau County.

  3rd graf: Caso is *not taking it lying down*.

  7th graf: Some say Margiotta has not enforced the peace because (1) he is *licking elective wounds*, (2) he is *gun-shy* from federal investigations of several Republicans and wants to *shed his boss image for a low profile*, or (3) he believes it's the right thing to do.

  10th graf: In the spring, he announced his availability, widely regarded as a move to force Caso's maneuvers *out of the closet*.

  No story can weather that many banalities. The last figure, incidentally, is not only a cliché, but a mangled one.
  Nor can a lead take off with this many bromides:

  LONDON (AP) — Few would argue that Britain is in what is often referred to as a bit of a pickle. A crisis in fact, undoubtedly of historic proportions.

- A cliché is acceptable when it serves your meaning precisely: *The city for years has tried to rid itself of these white elephants.* Never use a cliché as decoration or for emphasis; it has lost all power and glitter: *The rumor swept the town like wildfire.*

- Don't use a cliché as a facetious way to inflate a simple idea: *By the end of the year, the long arm of the law had caught up with him.* (*The law had caught up with him.*)

- When you must use a cliché, get it right. Don't *throw out the baby with the dishwater* (*bathwater*). Don't say, as a senator once did, that *we're all working like banshees.* (Banshees *wail.*) And don't make it, as a government secretary commenting on her boss's absence did, *when the wolf is away, the mice will play.* (Although that might have been a Freudian slip.)

- It's impossible to freshen a cliché, so let it slide past quietly without tinkering with it. *They put the fancy cart before the old horse* merely underscores the poverty of the phrase.

- Don't put clichés in quotation marks or apologize for them coyly with an *as the old cliché has it.* Inviting the reader to hold his nose just calls attention to the odor.

- Don't dress up your copy with Great Quotations that have been ground into the commonplace: *East is East and West is West and never the twain shall meet* (Kipling); *a rose by any other name ...,* the *slings and arrows ..., to be or not to be* (Shakespeare); *A rose is a rose is a rose* (Gertrude Stein). I hope to see one income tax deadline pass without a story reminding us that April is the *cruelest month* (T. S. Eliot).

- These and a hundred more, splendid in their original setting, have become debased currency by overborrowing.

- If there is one way to squeeze juice from a cliché, it's by twisting it to yield a new and surprising meaning: *Bedfellows make strange politics.*

SPORTS PAGE PARIAHS

Nowhere do clichés flourish more luxuriantly than on sports pages. It doesn't have to be this way, as good sportswriters prove every day. But the weaklings succumb in droves to the handy platitude.

There was a time when track teams were known, among other horrors, as thinclads, basketball players as cagers, tennis players as netmen, baseballs as horsehides and footballs as pigskins. If these have mercifully died out, they have plenty of replacements.

There may be no excuse for such littering, but there's an explanation.

The subject matter, for one thing, is pretty much the same. Stanley Walker, one of the great newspapermen of any year, summed up one part of the problem back in 1934 in his book *City Editor*: "Almost every murder, suicide, shipwreck and train collision is cut on a different pattern, and the reporter does not have to seek outlandish substitutes for common terms. One baseball game, however, is pretty much the same as any other. The few standard verbs and nouns used in writing of baseball, football and boxing become tiresome."

In short, as the event loses flavor, some reporters tend to overseason their prose; plain words like *defeat, win* and *score* seem wan and are swept away in a blaze of synonyms. The writer reaches for baubles, instead of relying on eyes, ears and insight, and unfortunately the baubles are the common property of the tribe. (Political writers slogging through a long, repetitive campaign face similar temptations. In fact, sports clichés are freely imported into politics: Look no further than the controversial horse race journalism.)

Second, some writers still treat sports as a mystical saga of superheroes, untainted by the ordinary grit and grime of human endeavor. That approach doesn't foster understatement. (Great sportswriters often have a soft spot for the more marginal athletes, who make it to the major leagues—barely—on effort and determination rather than an abundance of natural ability.) It also is not fair to the subject matter. The legendary Robert Lipsyte once noted that when you gild the lily in your words, "the flower dies."

Finally, there is the linguistic cannibalism in the closely knit world of sports, where writers, editors, coaches, athletic directors, players and publicists keep steady company and recklessly borrow from the sports pages and each other. As Walker said of the sportswriting during his early career, "Some of these words and phrases were pithy and effective. The trouble was that when one writer hit upon a good phrase the others took it up and used it until it became threadbare." The chewing of communal cud still produces a stream of new clichés every week without abandoning the old.

A crescendo builds with the fatuous questions and prefabricated answers at recurrent rituals: the locker room quotes, the pre-game and post-game meditations of coaches, the profound speculations of managers about World Series prospects ("We'll just have to score more runs than they do.").

There was a college football coach with a perennially losing team who had a card file with trite quotations that he consulted when talking to reporters. It's a wonder more of them don't, considering the bright sayings that keep tumbling into print:

> We just want the Eagles to respect us. They're playing for pride. If we can control the ball, we'll win. You've got to give them credit. We lost the momentum in the second half. Nobody can afford turnovers. They're a very physical team.

Writers are condemned to the cliché treadmill not by their subject matter, but by mental indolence. Red Smith wrote sports for nearly half a century until his death in 1982, but in his latter years you'd find fewer clichés in his copy than there are snakes in Ireland. "I have tried to become simpler, straighter and more pure in my language," he once said. "I look at some of the stuff I wrote in the past and I say, 'Gee, I should have cooled it a little more.'"

The writer who finds himself drifting toward the hotter latitudes, not to say the cliché doldrums, should cool it a little more.

We would then have fewer leads that tell us that "the Minnesota Vikings want to avoid home-grown players like the plague" or that baseball manager Jeff Torborg "has insisted all along—one game at a time." Or even:

> The Los Angeles Dodgers' pennant hopes are still full speed ahead even though they are stuck in reverse.

> "We've got our backs to the wall ..."

A fairly neat trick that, incidentally, did not win them the pennant. And we'd see more leads like this:

> The new model of the Big Red Machine won with spare parts. The Cincinnati Reds were so good in this World Series that they lost two-thirds of their starting outfield Saturday night and still swept the Oakland Athletics.

Perhaps someday we'll no longer see *athleticism, velocity, speed merchant, give their best shot, paint the corner, ring his bell, showed lots of heart, garnered* (goals, baskets, points), *collected wins, got off the schneid, down to the wire, legendary* (anybody in the Hall of Fame), *romp, blast* (home run) or *return artists*. But don't hold your breath.

Fifty years ago, Walker laid it out:

> The sports reading public today is remarkably well informed. It cannot be tickled by mere extravagance of writing. A lazy and incompetent writer finds it increasingly difficult to get by with a sloppy story, spun on a thread of artificial conceits. The demand is that he give his readers the facts, and give them straight. When crowds of 75,000 and more attend baseball and football games, and boxing matches, while millions more are listening on the radio, the sports writer should realize that he has an immense, well-informed audience that does not like to be fooled or short-changed.

And that was long before television increased the audience that can not only hear, but see for itself.

THE OVERREACHERS

Many clichés are metaphors and similes that have been worked to death but refused decent burial. Expert writers fluently devise their own, which helps make their language concrete and "picturable." But there are perils, too, in groping for novelties, and tyros tend to overreach themselves. Figures of speech are slippery characters, valuable when they're on target, distracting when they misfire.

The apt figure of speech has remarkable power; an example is Saul Pett's phrase that New York's baldish mayor Ed Koch "blushed like a kosher pumpkin," and, in a different vein, Jules Loh's metaphor in describing the arrival of a white whooping crane in a flight of drab sand cranes: "As the formation winged past the curtain of a mountain, the whooper appeared as a single glistening pearl in a pale gray strand."

Splendid images. Try for such phrases, but don't try too hard; a strained figure of speech is usually ludicrous, dismal or both.

In fact, when you're aglow with satisfaction over a newly hatched, unusual figure, give it a clinical second look. Such caution would have saved some embarrassment in the following newspaper examples:

> Interest rates are sprouting fresh skids today.

In a financial hothouse?

> His eyebrows followed in a tempestuous stare.

Most people stare, nontempestuously, with their eyes.

METAPHORS: MIXED AND PROTRACTED

Mixed metaphors are common misdemeanors:

> While the controversy is the latest storm to engulf him, it is the latest chapter in a long series of tangled events.

These are clichés, but a storm doesn't turn into a chapter.
A dead metaphor is sometimes brought to unseemly life by an active one:

> It was a rooted idea and it ran away with them.

Not unless you uprooted it first.

> His neighborhood, nestled east of Grand Concourse and south of Fordham Road, while remaining a womb of friends, family and fellow Italian-Americans, has suffered from police layoffs, an increase in burglaries, and the destruction or abandonment of apartment buildings.

A womb generally doesn't nestle, though something is said to nestle in a womb.

Worse, we're dealing with a giant and hyperactive womb.

Metaphors are sprinters, not long-distance runners. Know when to let go:

> Smith, an avid sailor, has been at the helm of his company five years, and during that time has steered it past many shoals.

> The worst squall he faced was a bitter proxy fight, but he weathered it and the seas have been calm since.

> In fact, the only one who makes waves now is Smith himself.

By the third paragraph, the reader needs a life preserver. Here's another protracted metaphor that should have been tackled before reaching the third graf:

> CHARLOTTESVILLE, Va.—For the University of Virginia's enthusiastic but inexperienced offensive linemen, the first weeks of the college football season will represent trial by fire.

> Will the searing heat of pressurized competition vaporize their pride and melt their competitive instincts, the way it did with their predecessors?

> Or will it instead transform them into a strong, resilient alloy? Their coaches and teammates are anxiously awaiting an answer—for the success or failure of the offensive line will likely determine whether the Cavaliers' season glows brightly or soon flickers into unfulfilled darkness.

THE PERSONIFICATION PERIL

Personification, with allegory, was the literary rage in the 18th century, but it goes against the modern grain and today is the feeblest of metaphorical devices. Language itself, of course, personifies: We say that luck smiles, fate frowns, and the like. But this is unobtrusive. Not so when we trot out Old Man Winter, Father Time or Mother Nature and endow them with human traits.

> Destiny's finger was about to tickle this man.

> Winter thrust his icy fist into the nation's mid-section today.

> He was riding high until Dame Fortune turned a cold shoulder.

> The mercury struggled all day to climb above zero.

Frankly, my friends, the mercury doesn't give a damn. Writing like this was on the wane when the weather service gave it fresh impetus with its disastrous decision to christen hurricanes. Some writers have found the temptation irresistible. Here's a milder example of what's done to our frolicsome tempests:

> The petticoat of hurricane Belle sashayed through New Jersey toward a landfall on Long Island today, buckling a four-block section of Atlantic City's famed boardwalk ...

Actually, if anything sashayed, it was Belle rather than her boardwalk-buckling petticoats, but it doesn't really matter.

OTHER POISONOUS MIXTURES

We've been considering verbal mishaps that shouldn't happen, but that carry no grievous consequences. It's different when, in chasing too hard after a clever, cute or poetic expression, a writer comes up with an incongruous analogy. Don't mix the important with the trivial, the serious with the silly. The brew can explode.

> BALTIMORE—The smoke has cleared from the Vatican's Sistine chapel, but the fire still smolders in the locker room of the troubled Baltimore Colts.

Equating a papal election with the intramural squabbles of a football team may be an original thought. But connecting two unrelated things makes a statement about each of them, which derails the entire lead.

> SLIPPERY ROCK, Pa. (AP)—Slippery Rock University Coach Bob DiSpirito doesn't worry his back-up kicker will improvise an ill-advised pass at an inopportune time, as Garo Yepremian once did in a Super Bowl.
>
> Bonnie West, you see, has no arms. Heart, yes; arms, no.
>
> SOUTH BERWICK, Maine (AP)—A man who caught an Atlantic sturgeon roughly the size of basketball great Wilt Chamberlain had the fish seized by the state, and could be sentenced to a year in prison and fined $1,000.
>
> The fish, at 7-feet-8-inches, was 6 inches longer than Chamberlain, and outweighed him by 25 pounds during the basketball star's playing prime.

Keep your critical faculties awake. Does this parallel make sense? Is that comparison far-fetched? That humorous sally offensive? The metaphor mixed? The simile comparing apples with oranges? Is it perhaps just a decorative cliché?

When in doubt, strike it out. Even apt figures of speech should be used sparingly; too many create a filigree that's out of place in the simple, direct style. As Strunk and White note in *The Elements of Style*, similes coming in rapid fire weary readers by asking them to compare everything with something else.

WORDS TO SWEAR AT

These clichés are among the dreariest in captivity, in one editor's opinion anyway. The list is not exhaustive. You may or may not find your favorite here:

armed to the teeth	drop in the bucket
banker's hours	fame and fortune
battle royal	feast or famine
beat a hasty retreat	fickle fortune
beauty and the beast	gentle hint
bewildering variety	glaring omission
beyond the shadow of a doubt	glutton for punishment
bite the dust	gory details
blazing inferno	grief-stricken
blessed event	Grim Reaper
blessing in disguise	hammer out (an agreement)
blissful ignorance	hand in glove
bull in a china shop	happy couple
burn one's bridges	head over heels in love
burn the midnight oil	heart of gold
burning issue	heavily armed troops
bury the hatchet	hook, line and sinker
calm before the storm	iron out (problems)
cherished belief	intensive investigation
clear the decks	Lady Luck
club-wielding police	lash out
colorful scene	last but not least
conspicuous by its absence	last-ditch stand
coveted award	leaps and bounds
crack troops	leave no stone unturned
curvaceous blonde	light at the end of the tunnel
dramatic new move	lightning speed
dread disease	limp into port
dream come true	lock, stock and barrel

long arm of coincidence (the law)

man in the street

marvels of science

matrimonial bliss (knot)

meager pension

miraculous escape

Mother Nature

move into high gear

never a dull moment

Old Man Winter

paint a grim picture

pay the supreme penalty

picture of health

pillar of (the church, society)

pinpoint the cause

police dragnet

pool of blood

posh resort

powder keg

pre-dawn darkness

prestigious law firm

proud heritage

proud parents

pursuit of excellence

radiant bride

red faces, red-faced

reins of government

rushed to the scene

scantily clad

scintilla of evidence

scurried to shelter

selling like hotcakes

spearheading the campaign

spirited debate

spotlessly clean

sprawling base (facility)

spreading like wildfire

steaming jungle

stick out like a sore thumb

storm of protest

stranger than fiction

supreme sacrifice

surprise move

sweep under the rug

sweet harmony

sweetness and light

tempest in a teapot

tender mercies

terror-stricken

tip of the iceberg

tower of strength

trail of death and destruction

true colors

vanish in thin air

walking encyclopedia

wealth of information

whirlwind campaign

wouldn't touch with a 10-foot pole

DOUBLEHEADERS

Lawyers love paired words with related meanings, like *null and void, part and parcel, aid and abet, sum and substance* and *irrelevant and immaterial*. They're kissing cousins of redundancies.

Leave such singsong pleasures to the barristers. When a doubleheader comes to you unbidden, as it usually does, pause to consider if one word won't say it all:

beck and call

betwixt and between

bits and pieces

blunt and brutal

bound and determined

clear and simple

confused and bewildered

disgraced and dishonored

each and every

fair and just

few and far between

nervous and distraught

nook and cranny

pick and choose

ready and willing

right and proper

safe and sound

shy and withdrawn

smooth and silky

various and sundry

Chapter 11

Features: A View from the Poets' Corner

The hard news story marches briskly through the whats, whens and wheres, looking neither right nor left, packing in enough details to give readers a clear picture.

In features, the immediacy of the event is secondary. The plain ladder of descending news values is replaced by human interest, mood, atmosphere, emotion, irony and humor. Features are usually connected to the news, but not driven by it; they represent a chance to get to know more about a person in a lot of stories, or a small sideline issue in a larger story that has caught the reporter's attention. If hard news is event-driven, features are best understood as writer-driven, an opportunity to use different storytelling tools to inform your reader.

The range of features encompasses the gourmet column and Orphaned Dog of the Week as well as news enterprise of major significance. New formats like the explainer or the fact-check have come into vogue in the past decade. The more compelling features supplement the straight news content in timely and topical ways: They illuminate events, offer perspective, explanation and interpretation, record trends and tell people about people.

Because features are less shackled to the moment than hard news stories, writers usually have more time to develop them. Proper use of that time takes a special discipline. Some writers, unfortunately, use it to lard their copy with clusters of adjectives, purple passages and other decorative devices. If you feel the decorative impulse coming on, lie down until it goes away. Strong feature writing is simple, clear, orderly and free of labored mannerisms and tricks that call attention to the writing itself rather than the substance.

FIRST, THE BEGINNING

Most hard news stories follow a basic pattern. By comparison, the feature floats free. The writer has the choice of many approaches. This offers splendid opportunities to the skilled and imaginative, but it also holds traps for the unwary, particularly in the first several paragraphs, the intro.

There's never any doubt about the point of a straight news story; the lead tells you. In features, that point may be postponed. You don't have to play it out explicitly in the first graf or two. But readers need to know soon what the story is about, and why they should go on reading; features are longer, so the reading time is a more considerable investment. Bury this crucial point too far beneath anecdote, description and atmospherics, and you'll exasperate readers rather than intrigue them. This is what happened in the following story:

> Come right in. Dinner will be ready in just a minute. Susie is making dinner tonight. You can hear her in the kitchen, talking to Connie Karli, who is in charge here.
>
> That's Connie's voice, telling Susie to make sure that none of the eggshells get into the bowl. Tonight, it's scrambled eggs, sausage and salad. It's slow going, with Connie steadily supervising.
>
> "You have to be careful with the shells," Connie says.
>
> "Why, Connie?" Susie asks, scrupulously scooping out eggshells with a fork. "Why do you have to be careful with the shells?"
>
> Susie is very cautious when she cooks; she takes great delight in serving a good meal, when it's over, but what she likes best is setting the table. Susie, who is 35, with dark hair and delicate skin, never cooked when she lived at home with her parents, but now she takes her turn making dinner.
>
> Since everyone moved in at 366 Highland Ave. the only major renovations have been in the kitchen, which is now filled with new appliances ...

The story continues for another long paragraph before readers are told they're visiting a home for people with developmental disabilities. Maybe you guessed that. Or in print you might have relied on clues from a picture or headline. But as a piece of writing, it simply does not get to the point.

The following intro sets a scene descriptively, but rambles through massed adjectives and generalities.

> HATTERAS, N.C.—The narrow road that threads its way northward along Hatteras Island from Hatteras Inlet to the village of Nags Head has been called one of America's most scenic drives.
>
> To the east, white-capped waves roll in from what early mariners knew as "The Graveyard of the Atlantic." Pamlico Sound, dotted with scores of fishing boats, sparkles to the west. Flocks of wild ducks and long-legged exotic birds perch on the high dunes along the road to Cape Hatteras National Seashore and Pea Island Wildlife Refuge.
>
> In the winter, the Outer Banks region is isolated except for the hardy native fishermen. Tourists don't venture onto the storm-swept islands until the summer warms up the 75 miles of beaches and the dozens of motels and restaurants open for the season.

Readers must plod through two more paragraphs of this travel-brochure prose until they are told that the "scenic and historic" Outer Banks, like other barrier islands, are threatened by erosion, the sea and the carelessness of man.

Equally unfortunate, the writer doesn't offer a single fresh observation of the wild beauties of the place but falls back on clustered adjectives: *scenic, white-capped, storm-swept, hardy, exotic*—words trotted out automatically for such occasions.

Next is the start of a piece on artificial life by AP Special Correspondent Nancy Shulins. She delays the transition to her main subject until the seventh graf, but it works because from the outset the reader is lured into an uncanny world that points in that direction:

> It's a dog-eat-dog world inside Danny Hillis' computer, home to 64,000 competing programs. Only the fittest will survive.
>
> Fitness, in this 5-foot universe, is the ability to sort letters alphabetically. But Hillis, its creator, doesn't teach his programs how to sort. Instead, he sets up a world in which programs with sorting ability are more likely to survive. Then he waits.
>
> The early programs are terrible sorters. The worst are killed off right away. Some put A before Z by blind luck, but that's good enough. They "mate," merging successful traits in "offspring" that do better still.

Evolution proceeds at a dizzying pace. The result, after 10,000 generations: "A better program for alphabetical sorting than anything I could write," says Hillis, a programmer with a doctorate from Massachusetts Institute of Technology.

There can be no doubt that software that evolved in Hillis' computer is superior to anything a human can produce.

The question is, is it alive?

Probably not—or as Hillis is apt to answer, not yet. But to him and other scientists on the frontier known as artificial life, it's only a matter of time before life becomes—literally— what we make of it.

Following is another anecdotal approach, from *The Associated Press*, which puts the effects of a political conflict on a country's residents into sharp relief.

CUCUTA, Colombia (AP) — For Anahis Alvarado, whose battle with kidney failure has become more desperate as Venezuela sinks deeper into crisis, the prospect of bringing in emergency medical and food supplies can't come soon enough.

She's watched five fellow patients in her dialysis group die over the past few years due to inadequate care. Only a quarter of the dialysis machines where she receives treatment at a government-run clinic in Caracas still work.

And last week she had to spend almost a third of her family's monthly income buying basic supplies like surgical gloves and syringes that President Nicolas Maduro's bankrupt government is no longer able to provide.

"We're losing time," the 32-year-old Alvorado said.

She hopes relief will soon be on its way.

This lead moves past the political stakes of a confusing and many-sided standoff to provide a picture of how the conflict affects real people. This moves past the abstractions and journalese of debates between politicians. Right after we get that introduction, the writer explains how this story fits into the overall conflict.

Some 620 miles (1,000 kilometers) away, in the Colombian border city of Cucuta, opponents of Maduro are hastily putting together plans with U.S. officials to open a "humanitarian corridor" to deliver badly needed food and medicine.

The aid convoy is seen as a key test for Juan Guaido after the opposition leader declared himself interim president in a high-risk challenge to Maduro's authority—a move that has the backing of almost 40 countries around the world.

But getting the food into Venezuela is no easy task. On Wednesday, a large tanker, mangled fencing and a shipping container were scattered across a bridge connecting the two countries, a makeshift barricade reflecting Maduro's longstanding rejection of outside assistance.

"We aren't beggars," the embattled socialist said Monday in a speech to troops.

The standoff has troubled international relief organizations, many who say the issue of humanitarian aid is being used as a political weapon by both sides.

The last paragraph here could function as a hard news lead.

CUCUTA, Colombia (AP)—International relief organizations said humanitarian aid was being used as a political weapon by both sides as conflicts over control of Venezuela's government continued.

That would seem acceptable as far as it goes, but is flat and dry in comparison with the anecdotal, storytelling method the writer chose. This, of course, is the special appeal of the feature story.

THE INTEREST IS *HUMAN*

One problem with the dehydrated lead is that it is general. Moving from the general to the particular is seldom as effective in feature writing as the other way around. A broad-brush opener tends to be duller, unless the writer is unusually lucky or adroit. Whenever possible, raise the curtain on a human actor and human action, not a juiceless stage setting.

If, for example, you start a report on the effects of the Cuban influx on Miami with an "overview" of the emigrés' influence on the city's economy, culture and politics, you're likely to wind up with an abstract catalog that lacks human interest. If, on the other hand, you start with an anecdote about an individual or family whose experience exemplifies one or more of these phenomena, the readers are instantly caught up in somebody's life. They'll follow that with greater interest than a sociology study.

Good feature writers capitalize on this and bring it off even where a particularized, human-interest focus seems hard to devise. A story about the country recovering from the 2008 financial crisis was almost too big to fathom, destined to be weighed down by statistics and dismally scientific pronouncements of economists. Eli Saslow of *The Washington Post* was a

Pulitzer finalist for a story that looked at this phenomenon through the life of a traveling salesman.

> He had always managed to find optimism in even the worst circumstances, and here was another chance: a heat advisory, 98 degrees and rising at 11 a.m., the hottest day of the year yet.
>
> "Thank you," said Frank Firetti, 54, as he walked out of his Manassas office into a blast of humidity in early June. "Thank you," he said again. "What a perfect day to sell a pool."
>
> He opened the trunk of his 2004 Toyota compact and changed into his selling outfit of slacks, a yellow polo and a silver wristwatch. He rubbed lotion on his face and sifted through six pairs of shoes before grabbing his dockside loafers. His goal was to arrive at a customer's house looking "out of the catalogue," he said—no traces of mud on his feet, no worry lines carved into his forehead, no indication whatsoever that sales at Blue Haven Pools had been plummeting for five years running and that a staff of 24 full-timers had dwindled to six.
>
> His job was to stand with customers in their back yards, suntanned and smiling, and look beyond the problems of the past several years to see the opportunities in every suburban cul-de-sac. How about a pool and a sauna next to the patio? Or a custom waterfall near the property line?
>
> "The possibilities here are as big as you can dream them," he liked to tell customers, gesturing at their yards.
>
> In a country built on optimism, Frank Firetti was the most optimistic character of all: the American salesman—if not the architect of the American dream then at least its most time-honored promoter. He believed that you could envision something and then own it, that what you had now was never as good as what you would have next. Since the country was founded, it had climbed ever upward on the spirit of people like him, on their vision, on their willpower, on their capitalism. But now, when he traveled from house to house to sell his monuments to American success, he sensed that spirit waning.

This introduction takes a generalized cultural image, the salesman, and gives him to us in all of his specifics. We can see how the stereotypes differ from the realities of this life on the road. It builds to the point of the story: have Americans really emerged from The Great Recession? Obviously, the data and stats underpin these questions, but in talking about something unquantifiable like American spirit, anecdotes may be more telling than data.

NO PRECOOKED DINNERS

The news story starts from an event. The feature story starts from an idea. "Let's do a story on the changes in Appalachia," the editor decides. "There haven't been any changes," the reporter discovers. "Fine, then let's do a story on why not. After all, the government poured millions into the place."

This is vague, but that's how it should be. Refining and massaging the idea is the outcome of, not the preliminary to, reporting. If the idea can travel virtually unchanged from your brain to the page, it either was not an interesting idea to begin with or the writer put on blinders to avoid seeing things that would complicate a planned narrative. The latter is the worst sin in feature writing. First, you will restrict your reporting from the outset to sources and material that fit your preconceived thesis. You may miss a far better angle. Second, and worse, you may miss what's really important and thereby distort the truth.

Start your reporting and interviewing with an open mind. In time, and by dint of legwork and research, the story will assume a natural shape. You may have wanted, say, to do the Appalachian piece from the perspective of state officials and welfare workers who administer government aid. You may find that three old ladies who were among the first food stamp recipients, all of whose children worked in the mines, can open up richer vistas. The point is, stay loose until you have enough of a feel to decide that you have the right theme. At that phase, you'll be able to narrow your reporting to its requirements.

At first, though, cast your net wide. You never know what facts and details, peripheral when you haul them in, will turn into treasure when you write. The fact that the mine inspector is a rose fancier is worth little—until you discover that the mine operator he's dragged to court shares the floral passion and has been bested twice by the inspector in a state flower show. You won't get such piquant detail, which gives your story vitality, unless your questions and your curiosity range well beyond the reservation of the immediate subject.

Since you'll need to reconstruct a scene, recapture mood and atmosphere, you might do well to follow the cherished practice of AP's Hugh Mulligan, a longtime feature writer turned columnist: "I find it helpful to copy down emotions, observations and passing thoughts on how I feel about what I'm witnessing or hearing, mainly because I may never feel that way again when I sit down to write," he has said. "I take endless notes on everything I hear and see and smell and think or moon about."

Because most good feature writers amass a far greater hoard of material for every enterprise than they can use, writing becomes a great winnowing. Writers often can't bear to part with an amusing anecdote, a character vignette or a nosegay of facts that are amusing and interesting. But do these things bear directly on the subject? If not, show them the door. Your profile of the single-minded engineer deals with his astonishing labors and the qualities of an infinitely precise mind that bring them about. His mother-in-law's odd experiences at a haunted house in Scotland are beguiling, but beside the point. Perhaps those details can turn into a side angle for a multimedia project—an additional piece of content that stands alone, though next to your feature. But for your feature, get rid of them. If you have three anecdotes illustrating the engineer's strange work habits, from midnight to eight in the morning, use the *one* that best makes the point. Don't belabor it with the others, however charming.

This process of selection is the feature writer's purgatory. The good ones go through it with every story, though never cheerfully. The harsh winnowing of the past was based on limited newsprint. It is tempting to forget about now that web pages have endless scrolling capacity. But we are writing for readers who expect engaging copy and most of whom will not keep pressing the space bar. As former newspaperman and college professor Don Murray put it: "Creativity is not the product of freedom, but the product of the conflict between freedom and discipline." The true craftsman can paint on a small canvas as fetchingly as on a large one.

Much agony can ensue from a craving to be definitive, which isn't the same as being thorough. Journalists, including feature writers, can never hope to say the last word on any subject. If you try that on a topic like climate change or the size of government or racial discrimination you're assailing Everest with your forehead. Limit yourself to a manageable slice of the subject. Your contribution will be all the more valuable for it.

A feature story needs structure. Like the Red River, it can take all sorts of bends and curves, but it always stays within the banks.

No offshoots flow from it. Readers should be able to follow it as if in a canoe, always curious about what's around the next bend.

CHRONOLOGICAL APPROACH

Chronological narrative, which kept Scheherazade alive, is the simplest structure and often remarkably effective, particularly in reconstructing large events like the September 11 attacks or a mass shooting.

While many features include chunks of chronology, they are usually modified by various devices. You may start in the middle of an action and use flashbacks. Always, you should spice straight chronology with fore-shadowing—teasers, hints of what lies around the bend.

In a story on the 100th anniversary of Franklin D. Roosevelt's birth, for instance, Saul Pett gave a largely chronological account of the president's mighty labors. But he framed the narrative in the experiences of two plain citizens whose lives had been greatly changed by the New Deal. (Direct tie-in with the present is a good practice in stories on historical subjects.) His format also gave Pett a human-interest intro, leading from the two individuals to the affairs of state, and an ironic ending: One of those old New Dealers' sons had voted for Reagan.

Structure need not be elaborate. You can build some stories from scenes, more or less connected, with or without narrative transitions, each high-lighting a significant episode. The "reporter's notebook" technique is a pleasant variant, informal and chatty, dipping rather than digging into a subject. It usually consists of separate items and vignettes, sketching vari-ous aspects of a place or event. The result can be highly readable, but suc-cess depends on sharp observation and good detail. And the pearls should be on a common strand, with some thematic relation among the items; you're not cleaning out the attic.

AP's Sid Moody devised a novel structure for a profile of New Jersey. The story was a dazzling almanac of facts—historical, contemporary, statistical, out-of-the-way, plainly odd—interspersed at times with nonfacts by way of humorous hyperbole. The format was a drive along the New Jersey Turn-pike, with Moody as the genial tour director, pausing at each exit to display the economic, physical and social landscape.

Here's how he began the story:

N.J. TURNPIKE (AP)—Standup comic: "Swine flu was discovered in New Jersey—where else?" (Laughter.)

Other Comic: "The Mafia is feeling the recession. They laid off four judges in Jersey." (More laughter.)

New Jersey today is an automatic boff, funnier than Brooklyn or downtown Burbank. The laughter emanates from the trillions of non-Jerseyans who cruise up the Turnpike staring at rear bumpers, dodging chemical trucks, sniffing refineries and gladly surrendering $1.50 to escape across the Hudson into New York.

It gets no respect. Yet Jersey gave America the steam locomotive (Hoboken, 1825); baseball (same place, 1846); football (New Brunswick, 1869); Edison's lightbulb (Menlo Park, 1879); movie cliffhangers (Palisades, early 1900s); the four-lane highway and cloverleaf (Newark); Count Basie; Valium; Meryl Streep; Allen Ginsberg; me and Secaucus. (Laughter.) And it may become a pioneer in what to do, and what not to do, about rotted cities, dwindling farmland, aging suburbs, regional planning and local government. It may just be where the country is going.

New Jersey is 7.3 million people; 5 zillion pickups; sixth among the states in per capita income; 300-plus garbage dumps with Jimmy Hoffa buried in every one; 150,000 deer; 12 armored divisions of Mafiosi; nine casinos; 16 skillion suburbs; 3,518 bartenders named Louie; one covered bridge; two U.S. senators, one a basketball player, the other convicted in the Abscam affair, and 40 of the state variety, three of them indicted. All of this acted out on a small stage.

A peek at the future? Turn off here, Exit 1.

Yup, that's a silo. We have 9,100 farms with about 1 million acres. They produce $2,977 per acre, tops in the nation. But half the farmland is owned by non-farmers. 'Read developers.' Jersey farmers, average age 53, have a morale problem with subdivisions crowding right into the barnyard. The new suburbanites complain about chicken feathers on the front lawns, about missing trains because they got stuck behind an 8 mph tractor. The Garden State grows only 54 percent of its vegetables. Milk comes from Wisconsin. The farmers sell out and retire to Florida.

Belatedly, New Jersey thinks this is no solution.

Without following Moody all the way to Exit 9, you might note two things:

An avalanche of facts and figures doesn't necessarily smother a reader. Moody's cornucopia gives his piece a special charm. Moody (a persistent, if flawed, trombonist on the side) is aware that sometimes there is music in mathematical preciseness.

The fifth paragraph performs a valuable service, crystallizing the significance of the story by relating New Jersey's condition to the nation at large. All sizable features benefit from such a "pregnant paragraph" high in the story, telling the reader: "Here's what's important (or unusual) about the story. Read on."

You may have caught Moody sneaking in a first-person pronoun ("me and Secaucus"). It is fine for this occasion as another humorous aside. But in general, leave the perpendicular pronoun to the columnists. The exceptions to this rule are rare—stories in which the writer is a character somehow, perhaps overcoming a debilitating illness or surviving three weeks in the Amazon garlanded with anacondas.

(An aside: The Big "I" is not essential to establishing a reporter's "voice." Skillful writers achieve the same effect through style, tone, irony, humor and imaginative phrasing.)

People are by definition human interest, or at least human, and profiles are a staple of feature output. They range from the full-fledged portrait of 2,000 words to more cursory sketches of someone in the news.

Don't cram a profile with routine biographical detail; keep that for the obit. Look for the characteristics, habits, traits, working methods and experiences that make your subject different.

In short profiles of "personalities in the news," it's a good idea to concentrate on qualities that got them there. If you're dealing with a person who has just ascended to high office in a major corporation, pick anecdotes, quotes and background details that help explain the success.

When you can, relate details and color to the main theme: *He wears a version of the same suit every day, preferring to save all his decision-making capacity for the office.* Or *In her gardening—her main hobby—she's as organized and meticulous as she's said to be in running the new division.*

Routine profile interviews of celebrities tend to be the least promising. That's because celebrities are acutely media-conscious, forever intent on their, Lord help them, "image." They have stock answers to all the usual questions and become vague or tongue-tied at unusual ones. They like people. They think the city they're in is wonderful. They like sports. They like music. They like babies. They like mothers. They think love is wonderful. They adore walking in the rain. They find everything a challenge. They are, in fact, animated clichés.

The best hope is to get such people to talk about their one vein of expertise or enthusiasm, if any; the actress may be interesting on acting techniques, the schlock author on how he trip-hammers his epics together. People know what is inoffensive in chit-chat, but when thinking about what they do every day, strong opinions tend to emerge.

Ask a plumber or a microbiologist about politics, theology or current affairs, and you'll usually get regurgitated opinions as fascinating as the telephone book. Let them discourse about the ins and outs of plumbing or microbiology and they're apt to wax voluble, enthusiastic and downright informative. Such stuff, even when slightly technical, usually is interesting even to readers without passion for pipe wrenches or electron microscopes.

Profiles of Very Important Citizens often require great effort to avoid the puffery fed you by the handiest sources—assorted aides, associates and flunkeys. Tapping Wilbur Lickspittle Jr. for quotes about his boss, Jarvis Housingstart, the Biggest Builder in the West, is unlikely to prove revealing. Balancing Lickspittle's fawning testimonial with the bleats of tenants at Housingstart Heights, where the roof recently blew off in a mild breeze, won't necessarily get you closer to the real Housingstart. You need sources who know him well but neither are beholden nor harbor a vendetta. It takes work.

WHERE SOLEMNITY PALLS

A sense of humor, an eye for irony and a light touch are formidable assets. You're thrice blessed if you have them. Not every subject can be treated lightly, but none calls for stodgy solemnity. The feature, after all, is intended to please as well as inform. A certain playfulness of style is seldom out of place. Saul Pett's epic on the bureaucracy, as you saw from the earlier sample, was relaxed and informal for all of its weightiness of subject.

Here's another example of Pett in full cry:

> NEW YORK (AP)—He is the freshest thing to blossom in New York since chopped liver, a mixed metaphor of a politician, the antithesis of the packaged leader, irrepressible, candid, impolitic, spontaneous, funny, feisty, independent, uncowed by voter blocs, unsexy, unhandsome, unfashionable and altogether charismatic, a man oddly at peace with himself in an unpeaceful place, a mayor who presides over the country's largest Babel with unseemly joy.
>
> Clearly, an original. Asked once what his weaknesses were, Ed Koch said that for the life of him he couldn't think of any. "I like myself," he said.
>
> The streets are still dirty. The subways are still unsafe. The specter of bankruptcy is never further away than next year's loan. But Edward Irwin Koch, who runs the place like a Jewish mother with no fear of the rich relatives, appears to be the most popular mayor of this implausible town since Fiorello LaGuardia more than a generation ago.

Yes, yes, elsewhere I extol the short sentence and especially the short lead, and this one runs 65 words. Which only means that when a good writer breaks a rule for good reason, it works. Anyway, the reader is having fun.

POETIC LICENSE FORBIDDEN

Feature writing, as the above lead demonstrates, offers greater latitude than straight news writing. It thrives on color, nuance, wit, fancy, emotive words, dialogue and character. Feature writers, like novelists, have many literary devices to engage readers emotionally, and that's their privilege.

But freedom, as has often been noted, entails responsibility. Feature writers must be accurate and scrupulously fair. Feature writers may be trying to access essential truths about people and institutions, but as journalists they work only with literal truths.

What you say happened must have happened in precisely that way. Frolic with words, enjoy yourself (if any writer can), but remember there's no poetic or literary license when it comes to facts. Repeat that to yourself every morning.

Fairness is more difficult to pinpoint, but a person can be sandbagged in many ways by the techniques in the feature writer's armory—through selection of details, through invidious description, through the use of adjectives and even through the setting of a scene.

That doesn't mean that every anecdote that presents a subject in an unfavorable light must be balanced by a favorable one, or that every critical comment must be offset by a burst of praise. Fairness is not a matter of arithmetic.

It does mean that feature writers, as honest reporters, recognize that life is multidimensional, that motives are often ambiguous, that moral judgments are beyond their purview and that a one-sided portrayal, whether of a person or an institution, is a sin even less pardonable than shoddy technique.

ARTISTS AT WORK

The best way to learn feature writing, or any writing, is to read—study—the work of those who know their business. I've drawn heavily on some of them in this section.

What follows is a small selection of features that repay reading and illustrate some of the points discussed. I wish space permitted a fuller representation.

The first is a story by the late Hal Boyle, irreplaceable dean of the AP Poets' Corner, reporter, Pulitzer Prize winner, war correspondent, columnist and master of the simple declarative sentence. The story is about the birth and death of a calf. Technically, it is a fine example of the power of understatement and of precise visual detail.

The second is a short profile of a retired revenue agent, by Jules Loh. It is obvious from the chosen material that Loh could have written at twice the length; he chose a smaller canvas. Note the economy of language. Every sentence is pertinent to the theme, every word tells.

My third exhibit, by AP Newsfeatures writer Jerry Schwartz, presents a remarkable profile of a severely handicapped man. He tells the story in a simple and direct style, strong on visual details and dialogue that add up to a rounded portrait.

They represent different categories of features, but note what all three have in common: Each is free of mannerisms, verbal flourishes, stylistic tricks and literary tinsel. Each demonstrates an unassailable truth: Good feature writing proceeds from good reporting.

Read and enjoy.

Life and Death in a Cow Barn
by Hal Boyle

LONG VALLEY, N.J. (AP)—It was an ordinary Sunday outside the big, cool dairy barn. The dressed-up people came and went to church, the less dressed-up people from the city enjoyed the sunny countryside.

Inside the big, cool dairy barn it was even more of an ordinary day. Cows have no Sunday. The daily drama of life and death among the herd went on unchanged except for one thing.

There was a young girl present who saw the drama for the first time. The events of the day changed her, perhaps forever. The three cows involved were numbered 204 and 140 and 219—and the first was old and through, the second was young and having her first calf, and the third was middle-aged and having maybe her third or fourth calf.

No. 204 was at the head of the barn and lying, too weary to get up, at the front of the barn with her head in its stanchion. She was 14, very old for a cow. Her milk had fleshed a thousand distant children she had never seen. But now she lay there, unprotestingly, waiting for the slaughterer's truck to come and take her away.

During the morning, No. 140, the young heifer, delivered her first calf after a rugged ordeal. Worn out by the struggle and oblivious to the responsibilities of motherhood, she wandered away from her sprawling, weak, tan calf.

A group of summer residents who came down to see the calf found that No. 219, the middle-aged cow, had taken up the duties of the confused young mother. She was carefully and methodically cleaning the sprawling calf with her tongue, as animals do.

Suddenly it became apparent the middle-aged cow's own ordeal of maternity was at hand. One of the men turned to a young girl, his niece, and said:

"If you're going to get back to the city before the traffic ties you up, you'd better leave now."

"I've never seen anything born before," she said. "I want to stay." "But it may be hours," he said. "You can't tell."

"Just for a little while," she pleaded. "Then I'll be off."

Her uncle and the others left and the young girl was alone in the filtered light of the barn, sweet with the deep rich scent of hay and animal bodies. Old cow No. 204, a factory worn out, glanced at her with the idle and placid disinterest of age.

The young girl knelt beside No. 219. The miracle of approaching birth made the two one. She knit her fingers and tugged at them tensely in unconscious rhythm with the laboring cow.

"Please," she whispered. "Try again, harder."

All at once they were three—or almost three. The calf was half-born. Then something was wrong.

"Please, please, please!" cried the girl. She heard a noise. Two dairy hands had come into the far end of the dairy barn.

"Quick!" she cried. "The calf is strangling."

The two men ran up. One grabbed a rope. With it they completed the rough obstetrics of the farm, and the calf was delivered, its forehooves raised to its muzzle in the posture of prayer.

The calf lay there—warm, wet and motionless. One workman bent and wiped its muzzle to clear the nostrils, then massaged its ribs in an attempt at artificial respiration. The calf lay still.

"But I saw its eyes move," said the girl. "If I could have called you in time ..."

The rough workmen looked at her, puzzled. A calf is $20, more or less, and they come often on a big dairy farm.

"I don't think so," said one of the men, not unkindly. "These things happen, you know."

As one of the men dragged the dead calf away, mother cow No. 219 let out a bellow of anguish that had a human ring of despair in it, and crashed into a chain barrier. She wandered about wildly for a moment, then lowered her head and again began licking the living calf of cow No. 140, the bewildered young heifer who hadn't yet risen to the chores of motherhood.

The young girl got into her car.

"But I saw its eyes move," she said, half crying. "If I could have just ..."

She turned the car and headed it toward the city. She had seen the sadness of death taking life at the portal of birth, and she would always remember this Sunday, just another ordinary day on a busy farm.

Big Six Henderson
by Jules Loh

LOUISVILLE, Ky. (AP)—In Kentucky's moonshine hollows, one name still strikes awe: Big Six Henderson.

Big Six Henderson busted up more stills in his time than anybody in history. If that is not so, at least it is the legend. When moonshiners talk about Big Six Henderson, the line between truth and legend blurs.

"I don't know what the record is," Big Six Henderson allowed, thinking back on his days of prowling around in alien corn.

"I know I raided more than 5,000 stills and sent more than 5,600 moonshiners to prison. You could figure it up. I've kept a copy of my daily reports for every day I was a revenue agent."

That was for a span of 28 years until he retired a few years ago, and it figures up to roughly a still every other day. The saga of Big Six Henderson, though, is hardly told in dry statistics.

The moonshiners Big Six Henderson tracked down imparted heroic dimensions to him and respected him as much as they feared him.

"Mr. Big Six," one woman said when he came to haul her husband off to jail for a third time, "we're proud to have folks know we know you." More than a few moonshiners named their children for Big Six Henderson.

One even named his mash barrel for him, painted "Big Six" on it and talked to it fondly.

"Good morning, Big Six," he said to the barrel one day. "Why don't we just run ourselves off a little batch, you and I. What do you say to that, Big Six?"

"That you're caught, Thurlow," Big Six Henderson said, stepping out of the mist.

At 75, Big Six Henderson is still impressive to behold. He is a bear of a man, 6-foot-4, with a thick bush of white hair and eyes the color of wet turquoise. His mother named him William; Big Six was the name he picked up when he was going to law school and throwing a baseball after the fashion of Christy "Big Six" Mathewson.

His career as a lawyer was as rapid as his fastball.

"My first and only case was defending a guy who broke into a warehouse. He was guilty as hell, but I got him off. I decided if I had to make a living that way I might as well be a holdup man and at least be honest about it."

There is nothing complicated about Big Six Henderson's sense of justice.

So he became a federal treasury agent, a "revenooer" as they are known in the hills, and went about it with a single-mindedness that became the stuff of myth.

Big Six Henderson can smell a still from 10 miles off. "Actually about two miles if the wind is right," Big Six Henderson corrected.

Big Six Henderson can shoot a pistol out of your hand at a hundred yards. "Well, the way that got started was by accident. I was aiming at the man's belt buckle."

It was no myth, though, that he could creep through the woods as quiet as smoke in his green raiding suit and could run like a deer for miles. Usually he didn't have to run after his quarry.

"Homer, halt!" he shouted at one fleeing moonshiner. The man froze in his tracks. "I'm halted, Big Six, I'm halted."

He was a legend in his time, all right, and not just because of his uncanny skill and his zealotry. He also had a reputation for fair play and decent treatment of the moonshiners he caught.

"I never regarded them as doing something evil, just illegal," Big Six Henderson said, "and I never abused them." The big man thumbed through a sheaf of his faded daily reports, looking wistfully at the names.

"Killed a few, but never abused them."

Churubusco's All-Round Nice Guy
by Jerry Schwartz

CHURUBUSCO, Ind. (AP)—Some days, John Krieger is a police officer, arresting bad guys. Some days, he is a fireman or a medic, saving lives.

Some days, he is an insurance agent. Some days, he helps out at the hardware store or at the barber's, at a restaurant or at the local paper. Some days, he preaches in church.

Always—as his business cards proclaim—he is "Churubusco's All-Round Nice Guy," appreciated not for what he does, but for what he is.

And this is what he is: A 63-year-old man with Down's syndrome, hobbled by weak eyes and aging legs, his words mumbled and hard to understand.

In other places, people might shy away from him, embarrassed by his tics and antics. But this is Churubusco, where John has spent his whole life. In this town of 1,800, 15 miles northwest of Fort Wayne, he is respected and cherished.

"What's not to like about him? I say when I grow up, I'll be just like him," says barber Norm Decker as he gives Wayne Haire a trim. "No chance of me growing up anytime soon, of course."

"John's all right. He tends to his own business," Haire says. "But look at how many businesses he's got," Decker replies.

Every day, John reports to work at Norm's or Diffendarfer's Body Shop or Shroyer's Variety & Hardware or any one of a half-dozen other businesses along Busco's Main Street. He helps out, tidies up, and they pay him $5 or $10 each week or just take him out for a soda.

But when you hire John, you give him more than a dust pan and a broom. You provide another platform for his fantasies.

On a recent Tuesday, John is helping with the stock at the hardware store when he bolts for the door. He races next door, into the office of the Churubusco News, and back to the garage.

He speaks excitedly into an imaginary police radio in his hand and then begins, with elaborate pantomime, to make an arrest.

"Take him to jail," John says.

Back in the newspaper office, Managing Editor Viv Rosswurm asks John what's going on. He explains that someone had been shot twice in the heart with a shotgun. Receptionist Marcia Hoffman expresses surprise.

"Monday's usually the killing day," she says.

John is always finding ways to bring excitement to the newsroom. The other day, Ms. Rosswurm says, John reported that "somebody in Fort Wayne came here and left this baby. I hate it when they do that."

Folks in Churubusco are used to John's police work; for many years, John would ride his bicycle up to the elementary school every day during recess, and would make an arrest.

In those days, the townspeople used to get together every so often to buy John a new bike and doll it up with lights. This was his squad car, and when he encountered a perp— perhaps someone who made an illegal turn—he would uncork an uncanny imitation of a siren and pull them over.

"We had a lot of startled strangers," Ms. Rosswurm says.

Then "traffic got a bit heavier, and his eyes got bad," says Doug Arnold, who works with John at the hardware store. John was knocked off his bike a few times, and an ambulance picked him up. "He wasn't hurt. He liked the excitement, the lights," says insurance agent Chuck Jones.

So a few years ago, they took his bike away. Now, he must do his police work on foot.

John's obsession with policing comes from his father—"a flatfoot," John says, who worked part-time as a Churubusco cop.

When John was born, doctors told his parents to send him to an institution. He might live to see his 14th birthday, but not much more, they said. He would be a burden. They would be better off without him.

Never, his parents said.

"That was their baby. They weren't going to give him up," says his sister, Beverly Davis. "One of your own, you don't send him away."

If he had been born today, Davis says, he might have received more training, and he might have learned how to be self-sufficient. Instead, he came into a world where little was expected of people like John, who were dismissed as Mongoloids.

When John was 20, he began to walk into town each day. Clarence Raypole, who owned the Standard filling station, took a liking to him and put him to work. Then the guy who owned the Ford garage, directly behind the gas station, asked John to help out.

Raypole died some time ago, but over the years, other merchants would take his place. "They just looked after him," Davis says.

When a tornado slammed through Churubusco—and John was out in the storm—his family was terrified.

"But we knew somebody was uptown, taking care of him," Davis says. Sure enough, another worker at the gas station crouched with John in the attendant's booth until the winds died down.

John lived with his mother, Hazel, until she died in 1989, and then with his sister, Phyllis. But when she died, two years ago, the calls started coming into the Churubusco News.

"What's going to happen to Johnny?" they asked. "Don't let the state take him," they pleaded.

They needn't have worried. His nephew, Don Ferguson, took him in. "If John was put in a home, if he was put to where he couldn't get out to do things, he wouldn't last that long," says Phyllis Ferguson, Don's wife.

He has his own room; it is extraordinarily neat. He keeps his prize possessions there, including his autographed picture of Purdue University basketball coach Gene Keady ("If you want to make him mad, just say something bad about Purdue or the Chicago Cubs," says Don Ferguson).

He makes his own breakfast, and then each weekday morning he walks to John Diffendarfer's body shop, arriving promptly at 9 a.m. He sweeps the floor, puts the tools in their place, takes out the trash.

"When we had that last snowstorm, he couldn't make it in," Diffendarfer says. "It got pretty messy here."

At 11:15 a.m., when John departs for home and a shower, the Rotary Club prepares for its weekly gathering in the St. John Bosco Church basement.

They sit down to ham, macaroni and cheese and Jell-O, and then they open the meeting with songs—"It's a Small World" and "Smile"—and a prayer. Visitors are asked to say a few words, and plans are made for the big auction, to raise money for scholarships.

This is truly small-town America. And Joe Dickson, the club's president, says "the smallness of the community, the town, everybody knowing each other," partly explains why John Krieger is embraced.

But there's more to it than that. Chuck Jones, a former Rotary president, says, "Johnny reaches out to you. There's many times when I've had a bad day, and Johnny comes in at quarter of five and lifts me up."

"He's kind of the town's soul, the town's heart," he says.

He's relentlessly upbeat. His playfulness is contagious; in his guise as a medic, he often stops in to give workers imaginary inoculations.

Who named him "Churubusco's All-Round Nice Guy"? "Me," John says, with a grin that shows off his single tooth.

He used to direct traffic at funerals. He still goes to most funerals; he writes "JOHN" in simple block letters in the register.

"He is THE man about town," says Greg Childs, director of Sheets Funeral Home. "John is absolutely a gift to us. It's his outlook on life. He's so positive. He always finds the good in people."

He has always watched out for children. "He was on our butt every day," remembers police officer Chad Fulkerson, 27. "If you didn't cross at the cross-walk—you used to yell at us, didn't you?"

John grins again, and rubs the gray stubble on his head.

He is drinking a Diet Coke with Fulkerson and officer Clifford Smith (together, two-thirds of a police force that made five felony arrests in all of 1998) and Sheriff's Deputy Tony Helfrich.

Cliff is John's best buddy. Every day—during his afternoon break, and before John goes off to one of his many jobs—Cliff picks him up in his squad car and takes him to the Ramble Inn.

John shows off his honorary sheriff's deputy card. The cops have given him a police radio with a limited range, tuned to frequencies only they can pick up. His handle is "Sarge."

Around the table, they kid John unmercifully. They ask him how many girl-friends he has (244, he says). They call him "Knothead" and "Fatboy."

"You got a piano case for your casket yet?" asks Cliff.

"They're treating him as an equal," says Pastor Dennis Shock. "It's like they're talking to their brother or their best friend."

Shock is minister at the Churubusco United Methodist Church, where John worships—or, more accurately, where John preaches. Every Sunday morning, before the 10:30 service, John climbs to the pulpit.

Many in the congregation—Shock included—cannot understand what he is saying. Soon after Shock's arrival in Churubusco four years ago, he heard complaints from some congregants who found it hard to meditate, and were afraid of what visitors from out of town would think.

Shock was not happy, either.

"He kept getting longer and longer, and a bit louder," Shock says. "Occasionally, I got worried that he wouldn't sit down."

So Shock approached John and suggested that he retire. The next Sunday, John did not preach. But the Sunday after that, Shock recalls, "there he was again, preaching as usual."

Shock gave up. Obviously, there was little he could do to dissuade John from sharing his special version of the Gospel. Besides, he had heard from congregants who LIKED having John on the pulpit.

"He knows about Christ and he prays. He knows what the Bible is and he believes in God. I know that much," Shock says.

"He's John," the pastor says. "He sort of ties this community together, in a way. They've all adopted him as their son, or father. I've never seen anything like it, and I've been in a few small towns."

His adopted family worries about John as he gets older; he had a mild heart attack not long ago, and he had surgery for cataracts.

Long ago, before antibiotics, a child with Down's syndrome was not expected to live to his teens. Now, the average life expectancy is 55, though many—like John—live longer.

In some ways, his life has become richer in recent years. Since he moved in with his nephew, new vistas have opened: The family sometimes eats out, and he likes that. And he went with them to Pennsylvania.

They drove at night, figuring he would sleep, but he did not close his eyes. "He didn't want to miss a minute," Ferguson says.

His birthday, each April, is a major event. "We keep telling him Marcia's going to jump out of a cake. He's all for that," says Ms. Rosswurm, editor of the News. Marcia, the receptionist, shakes her head vehemently.

Then, in June, comes the other high point of John's year: Turtle Days.

Fifty years ago, Churubusco had a moment in the spotlight. There were reports that a 500-pound turtle—nicknamed Oscar—had been sighted in a local pond, and the national media picked up on the story.

Oscar never surfaced. But they still call Churubusco "Turtle Town, USA," and they still have Turtle Days and the Turtle Parade every year.

And every year, "Churubusco's All-Round Nice Guy" rides a fire truck and waves to his 244 girlfriends, his fellow policemen, his flock, his many employers and all the men, women and children who are his friends.

"When Johnny's buried," says Chuck Jones, "it's going to be the biggest funeral this town's ever had."

Chapter 12

Usage: Handling Those Hectoring Hangups

SPLIT 'N' POLISH

Split infinitives were good enough for William Shakespeare, George Bernard Shaw and a flock of other capable writers. They should be good enough for the rest of us.

Shaw, in fact, once complained to a newspaper about the harrumphings of an anti-splitter.

"Your fatuous specialist," GBS fumed, "is now beginning to rebuke 'second rate' newspapers for using such phrases as 'to suddenly go' and 'to boldly say.' I ask you, sir, to put this man out without interfering with his perfect freedom of choice to suddenly go, to go suddenly, and suddenly to go. Try an intelligent Newfoundland dog in his place."

The only rule in writing is that there are no truly inviolable rules. Split for good reason: when it sounds better, and when it's to avoid ambiguity.

Some perfectly good splits:

> He embraced conspiracy theories *to really understand* what the government was up to.

It works because you can hear a conspiracy theorist saying it this way; perhaps it also encapsulates the sloppy thinking.

> The cops wanted those youngsters *to really see* the danger.

Painless split here that increases emphasis. Of course it only does this if we decide to split sparingly.

On the other hand, there's no point in splitting the infinitive here:

> The company hopes *to substantially increase* profits.

... *increase profits substantially* gets the nod. From the ear.

> They promised *to at all times* obey the law of the land.

They promised at all times to obey the law of the land is possible, but ... *law of the land at all times* seems preferable.

In general, it's best to avoid splitting an infinitive with two or more words.

> They planned *to quickly and decisively deal* with the economic slump.

Let's not buy that one. ...*deal with the economic slump quickly and decisively* sounds better.

> They suggested that Republican leaders have refused *to attempt seriously to solve* the Social Security problem.

Murky. *Seriously* might be read as modifying *to solve*. By all means, split: ... *to seriously attempt*.

Sometimes, it's impossible to avoid a split:

> The chairman expects the company *to more than double* revenues.

Where else could you put that *more than double*?

One way to avoid splitting an infinitive is with *not, never* or *always*, any of which goes more naturally beforehand:

> The mayor asked strikers *to not insist* on the march (change to *not to insist*).

> The president made sure *to always receive* his visitors at the entrance (preferable: *always made sure to receive*).

> At the meeting, he advised parents *to never let* the youngsters walk alone (*never to let*).

I hope this is enough to somewhat clear the air.

GENDERLY SPEAKING

The point can't be overemphasized: Words must fit together naturally, comfortably, so they do not distract the reader by calling attention to themselves. In the effort to rid the language of male bias—a commendable effort—distraction often results. Nowhere is the straining for fairness more contrived than in the juggling of personal pronouns.

> The mayor warned every homeowner that he or she is responsible for clearing the snow in front of his or her house.

To avoid implying all homeowners are male, the writer danced awkwardly around the problem, kicking up clouds of clutter. In this case, and most like it, the solution is easy. Recast the sentence to use the sexually neutral plural pronoun:

> The mayor warned all homeowners that they are responsible for clearing the snow in front of their houses.

The baby who sucks his thumb can as clearly and naturally be written *babies who suck their thumbs. A reporter tries to protect his sources can,* eliminating bias, become *reporters try to protect their sources.*

Understandings of gender change faster than language. As writers our responsibilities are accuracy and clarity. The *AP Stylebook* tells us to avoid presumptions of maleness whenever possible. Be especially alert for such constructions as *the boss ..., he,* which implies that only males are bosses. At the same time, avoid straining for neutrality through constructions that jar and call attention to themselves. As for nouns, apply the same rule. When the choice is a natural one—*reporter* for *newsman, firefighter* for *fireman, worker* for *workingman, mail carrier* for *mailman*—use the word that includes both sexes. For years AP rejected *spokesperson,* but now will use it if it is the preference of the individual being quoted.

That said, we increasingly know that gender binaries also should not be presumed. The pronoun *they* is what we use if that is the source's expressed identity. From a clarity perspective, it is better to rely less on personal pronouns in this case because some readers will be unfamiliar with *they* as a singular pronoun. Right now, the *AP Stylebook* also rejects other emerging gender-neutral pronouns, though that likely will change.

SUBSTITUTIONS: TERMINAL AND INCIPIENT

The old superstition, based on a grammatical fallacy, that no sentence should end with a preposition is happily dying out. For that matter, most good writers down the ages have ignored it.

> *Police recovered the bloody ax he killed her with* is good English, whereas *Police recovered the bloody ax with which he killed her* is stodgy.

As Winston Churchill said, it's a "pedantry up with which we will not put."

Some traditionalists also cling to another myth: Sentences must not start with *and* or *but*. No reason why they shouldn't, though in practice it's often overdone. Look over the initial *ands* and *buts* you write. And see if they are superfluous, as the *and* is in this sentence.

But implies a contrast, and for that reason—not because of its position— it is wrong here:

> The defendant appeared dejected by his wife's outburst. But the prosecutor indicated he might recall her later.

An *and* would be possible, but actually neither is needed.

IT'S ALL RELATIVE

Careful writers insist on correct use of the relative pronouns *that* and *which*, not merely out of respect for syntax but in the cause of clarity. The two words are used in restrictive and nonrestrictive clauses, respectively, and are not interchangeable. The following two sentences do not mean the same thing:

> The bicycle that was on the porch was stolen.

> The bicycle, which was on the porch, was stolen.

The first sentence restricts the sense to one specific bicycle—the one that was on the porch. In the second sentence, the fact that the bike was on the porch is incidental, peripheral and nonrestrictive. Such clauses, which can be dropped without harming the sentence, are always enclosed by commas unless they fall at the end of a sentence. Then, you need a comma only before *which*.

> The senator said the letter that disturbed him was received yesterday morning. (Restrictive—one particular letter is meant.)

> The senator said the letter, which disturbed him, was received yesterday morning. (Nonrestrictive—the senator's uneasiness is considered incidental.)

LEGALISM

And/or is something that lawyers seem to enjoy. It's one of those charming phrases that make legal forms so attractive.

Leave it to them. It's always avoidable:

> The officers thought they would find the loot and/or other evidence at the scene. (Use either *and* or *or* but not both.)

> The force was to consist of National Guardsmen and/or state police. (National Guardsmen or state police or both.)

Attorneys, in the ritual of avoiding leading questions and/or (chuckle) the appearance of prejudgment, fling themselves at *if any*. Some news writers are impressed by the sound, though it rarely makes sense in copy:

> There was a question of what effect, if any, the company proposal would have on the rank and file.

No effect is still an effect, so we can omit *if any*. If you want to quibble about that, there is still another way: *...if the proposal would have any effect ...* Here's a case where a reporter was more lawyerly than the lawyers:

> None of the lawyers involved would say what legal strategy, if any, they would take.

Candidates for disbarment, I'd say, if there's a chance that they would not adopt any legal strategy.

SUBJUNCTIVITIS

Writers sometimes tense up about describing things before they happen and flee into the "woulds."

> Still, McEnroe did not concede the third set. As he *would* say later, he had opportunities to win throughout the match.

There's nothing incorrect about the subjunctive construction, but why not make it *as he said afterward*?

The *woulds* thicken menacingly in this lead:

> MEXIA, Texas—The party would go on all night. But at 11 p.m., as the festivities were just gathering steam, the drownings that would mar memories of the day and create a furor whose tremors would reach Washington were about to happen.

That lead creates an eerie backward-forward-not-yet effect, and it isn't helped by the dreadful gulf between *drownings* and *were about to happen*.

The following gets us out of the time warp:

MEXIA, Texas—The party went on all night and was just gathering steam when the drownings occurred. Later, the tragedy marred the memories of the day and raised a furor whose tremors reached Washington.

If the extended subjunctive seems a clumsy way to grapple with the future, the fatuous backward glance seems even worse. The following makes much too much of the fact that the future is unknowable:

Little did Joe Smith know, when he peered shortsightedly at the blackboard in first grade, that he would someday be Smithtown's leading ophthalmologist.

That is a hypothetical example, but representative. Here is an actual example from a newspaper:

When Sidney Sheldon was writing his latest best seller, he probably had no idea it would be used as a challenge by those who have been saying that the Washington County library in Abingdon is loaded with dirty books.

The absurdity is compounded by the cautious *probably*.

You would do well to avoid the subjunctive if you can, and to leave speculative flashbacks alone altogether.

DASH IT ALL

A lot of writers like to toss around dashes to keep things stirred up. They look, well, more dashing than the crooked little comma, the hangdog semi-colon and the rotund parenthesis, for all of which dashes are frequently misused.

The comma indicates a slight break in the thought of a sentence; the semicolon a rather larger one, and the dash an abrupt, dramatic turn. Dashes, therefore, should be used sparingly; overuse weakens their effect. They often add a jarring note to an otherwise smooth sentence.

The dash is used correctly here:

They trudged wearily along the trail—dozens had died on it, and they knew it—until they made camp utterly exhausted.

But not in the following examples:

He said his grandmother—who had just reached 93—was a "very vigorous old lady."

No abrupt break in the thought. Use commas instead of dashes.

The defendant said he hadn't known she had left—without explanation.

Fake dramatics; change to ... *had left without explanation.*

> The 4,372-piece set—an average $48 per piece—had arrived at the White House by truck from the Lenox China plant.

Substitute parentheses or commas.

> Their arrival meant that suburbia—which has sprawled slowly across North Jersey since the 1930s—had finally pierced the state's westernmost farming country.

Use commas.

> The burden of clerical rule—including the banning of alcoholic beverages, Western music and movies; requirements that women be veiled, and Islamic punishments, including death for what are deemed sexual offenses—has fallen most heavily on the Westernized, the educated, and the middle class.

The dash must have looked to the writer as the only way to save this sentence. Had he tried parentheses or commas, he might have realized that he needed to go back to the drawing board.

LAY ON, MacDUFF

Despite the twanging testimony of country singers, it is possible to use *lie* and *lay* correctly.

I suspect the confusion stems from the fact that *to lay*, meaning "to place something on a surface," is also the past tense of *to lie*, meaning "to recline." To make matters worse, *to lie* is also the verb that means "to tell a falsehood," an inflammatory word that may cause some to flinch and use *lay*, incorrectly, in its place.

Lay aside, for a moment, the falsehood meaning of *lie* and concentrate on the two verbs that are so often confused. Start with the principal parts:

Verb 1—*lie, lay, lain*
Verb 2—*lay, laid, laid*

> The man stumbled to the park to *lie* on a bench. He selected the same bench that he *lay* on yesterday. He has *lain* on the same bench every night for the past week.

> He looked for a place to *lay* his knapsack. He *laid* it beside the bench in the same place as yesterday, the same place he has *laid* it for a week.

Remember: *to lay* takes an object; *to lie* does not.

ET CETERA

At the end of a sentence containing a string of words or phrases separated by commas, writers sometimes feel compelled to attach a meaningless little tail designed to tell the reader, "This is an incomplete list."

> The adult education program offers a wide variety of courses, such as woodworking, French cookery, creative writing and origami, *among others.*

> He stays active during his leisure hours with golf, carpentry, birdwatching, fishing, hiking *and similar activities.*

There's a way out of that hangup. In the first example, delete the *and* before the final item on the list and insert a comma: *... cooking, creative writing, origami.* In the second example, just cross out *and similar activities.*

The simple trick of omitting *and* before the final item in a list suggests it is an incomplete list. Read it aloud and you will see.

NUMBERS GAME

Numbers go into stories for precision. The way they're often handled, though, makes them sorry figures—vague and confusing enough to have readers muttering to themselves.

Let us count the ways:

1. The More-Less Seesaw

> Johnson got *more* than $100,000 *less* than he expected.

First, try to get an exact figure. (We hide too often behind approximations.) Failing that, write it this way: *Johnson expected at least $100,000 more than he got.*

> Fewer than the more than 60,000 ticketholders showed up.

Better:

> At least 60,000 bought tickets, but not all of them showed up.

> The staff of the state Utilities Commission recommended a $4.7 million rate hike for Carolina Telephone & Telegraph Co. But the recommended figure is more than $21 million less than the company expected.

I suspect one more phone call would have gotten the reporter the exact sum. Otherwise, *at least* is again the way out.

2. Mathematical Leads

> A jury of four men and eight women deliberated more than 21 hours before convicting a 19-year-old high school dropout of killing his 18-year-old girl-friend two years ago.

Too much. Stats-happy sportswriters also are prone to throwing curve balls:

> The rangy, 6-foot-6 forward who just turned 20 scored 22 points to Tibbets' 18 as the Jays pulled out the game with eight seconds to go for their 10th straight victory. They had trailed 34-33 at halftime.

> KANSAS CITY, Mo.—Nick Lowery kicked field goals of 20, 20, 42 and 41 yards Sunday, leading Kansas City ...

3. Bottomless Pit

> The company's losses could total up to $11 million ...

Or, as little as $2.50? Try to give the range: *The company could lose from $6 million to $11 million.*

4. Math Test

> When they first met, Klipstein was nearly twice the younger man's age.

And how much was that? Klipstein's age was given five grafs earlier. The younger man's age was never given.

> This was about two-thirds the amount they spent for food.

This story made the reader backtrack four grafs to find the food budget, then figure the two-thirds.

5. Execrable Approximations

About, almost and other fudges are sometimes necessary (don't write *approximately* or *some*), but they're best used with round figures only.

> *About* 112 policemen were sent to the scene of the disturbance.

Again, the best solution is *at least.*

> *More than* 13 people were in the group, and police seized *some* three.

The reader wonders why the reporter couldn't have gotten such a low count right. Otherwise, fall back on *at least.*

And don't say *about* when the number is exact and should be ascertained for the story: "... who handles newsprint purchases for the Gannett group of *about* 80 newspapers." No. Use the exact number. To do otherwise is just lazy.

6. Do the Arithmetic

When editing a story with numbers in it, double-check the writer's arithmetic. If the story enumerates groups of various sizes, for example, make sure the numbers add up to the figure in the lead. In short, do the math.

THAT'S THAT

Some sentences read well without *that*, others don't. There's no rule about when to put it in. It is true, though, that you can never go wrong by including it, while you can cause small disturbances by omitting it.

There's no problem with the absence of *that* in these sentences:

> The commissioner said she was sure they would comply. The secretary disclosed he would leave for Paris tomorrow.

There's something wrong with the following, however:

> Mayor Koch said years ago, the city had tried this method of financing but had failed.

That reads at first blush as though the mayor had said it years ago. *That* after *said* would have been better.

> He said in a survey of state motels by the state association, it was discovered ...

Again, use *that* after *said*. He didn't say it in a survey.

You must always use *that* when the word following a verb may be wrongly construed as its object:

> The teacher reported the children who threw the books would be disciplined.

> The committee vote signaled the bill stands a good chance of passing.

Without *that* after *reported* in the first example and *signaled* in the second, you have the teacher reporting the children and the vote signaling the bill. The reader is momentarily misled. Insert *that* after the verb to keep the meaning clear and the writing smooth.

It's usually better to use *that* when a time element comes between the verb and the *that* clause:

> The agency said today it will have additional shipments en route.

Slightly awkward, and the *today* may be briefly taken to refer to the shipments.

> Stephens said he would like to seek a compromise with Williams before taking the bill up in his committee because he believes the House of Delegates would approve the bill as before, but it is of little value if it is destined to die in the Senate.

This seems to require a *that* after the *but*, since the clause otherwise reads like the reporter's comment. A *that* in this second clause would also call for a *that* after *said*. A *but that* or *and that* in the second clause needs a parallel *that* in the first.

WHAT'S IN IT FOR ME?

Science writers and others on specialty beats know that part of their job is to translate—to reduce the vocabulary of, say, genetic engineering to lay terms. Covering legislatures and government usually doesn't entail such mysteries, but there are other hangups. Jargon, dealt with elsewhere, is one. So is an obsession with mechanics.

A common pitfall for legislative reporters is the notion that readers share the insider's passion for procedural detail and political shadow boxing. What readers want to know, right off the bat, is what's in it for them— the practical consequences. Legislative coverage and other governmental reporting that loses sight of this is writing tailored to the reporter's press-room pals, cloakroom pols and agency moles.

Note how blurry the one point of reader interest becomes given the inconsequential mechanics:

BOSTON—The Massachusetts Legislature has finalized action on a bill providing for a public vote in the November election on the question of repealing the state's Sunday closing laws.

By a voice vote, the Senate enacted the bill Monday and sent it to the governor. The last obstacle to the enactment of the bill was removed when the House, on a 178-33 roll call, voted not to reconsider its enactment of the passed bill several weeks ago.

The measure provides for a nonbinding referendum on the blue laws, which require that most business activity cease on Sunday.

BOSTON—The Massachusetts Legislature has decided to give voters a chance to state whether they want the state's blue laws repealed.

Under those ancient statutes, dating to colonial days, most businesses must be closed on Sunday.

The voters' verdict in November will not be binding on the Legislature. Business generally favors repeal, while some unions oppose it.

The Senate passed the bill setting up the referendum and sent it to the governor Monday. A move to block the measure in the House failed.

The right-hand version focuses on the substance of the legislation, while the original emphasizes procedure at needless length.

BISMARCK, N.D.—The 44th Legislative Assembly convenes Tuesday for the opening of what most legislative leaders have called one of the most important sessions in the state's history.

Few care what legislative leaders call it. More to the point is material that doesn't come up until the fourth paragraph:

BISMARCK, N.D.—The Legislative Assembly opening Tuesday will have to deal with the largest budget in North Dakota history and grapple with decisions about coal development in the western part of the state.

The following was intended mainly as a human (or animal) interest story. Why encumber the lead with legislative detail?

WASHINGTON—Members of a House-Senate conference committee agreed today on a legislative package for western ranges that includes provisions for giving away wild horses and burros to anyone willing to care for the animals.

WASHINGTON—If you want a wild horse or a burro, just promise you'll take good care of it and it's yours, courtesy of Congress.

In short, don't put the cart before the burro.

Chapter 13

BESTIARY: A Compendium for the Careful and the Crotchety

Standards of written English are not rigid. Some usages blossom briefly and die; others take root and enrich the language. The process is slow and unpredictable. Meanwhile, careful users of the language often disagree on this or that locution.

That said, what follows is a collection of usages that I regard as bestial. (In the matter of misuse of words, I allow myself to overstate.) Some of the entries, at this stage in the development of the language, allow for no argument. If you write *disinterested* when you mean *uninterested* you are wrong, period. Other entries, I admit, may be open to discussion—but not if I'm handling the copy. Every editor has crotchets. Among these are some of mine.

A BEFORE H. Unless you're prepared to write *an* horse, *an* ham or *an* hamburger, make it *a* historian, *a* historical or *a* hysterical moment. The initial H in those words is pronounced, or rather aspirated, unlike in *hour* or *honest*, either of which takes *an*.

ACCESS (as a verb). When you're trying to access a computer file or a website, the verb is in the right place. But leave it there. Never write, "The police accessed the building through a first-floor window." In ordinary (nontechnical) usage, the words are *entered, got in, gained entry*, and the like. (See INPUT.)

ACTIVE CONSIDERATION. Have you ever heard of anybody giving a plan or proposal passive consideration? This is bureaucratic baloney meant to sound grander than *thinking it over.*

AD HOC. Latin for "toward this." An *ad hoc* committee is one appointed to deal with one particular case or problem. Officialdom loves to go off ad hocked, and so does the business world. But why? If you write, *The league appointed a committee to oversee the flower show,* the *ad hoc* is understood. Or, you could say, *a special committee.* Use something other than *ad hoc—* at least *pro tem.*

ADDRESS (as a verb). A favorite pomposity of academia now spread like a fungus. *Address* a letter. Don't address a problem. Instead, *deal with it, take it up, consider it, tackle it* or *cope with it.*

ALTERNATELY/ALTERNATIVELY. Don't confuse the two. The first means "by turns": *They traveled alternately by snowmobile and dogsled.* If only one were available, they would go by dogsled, or, *alternatively,* by snowmobile.

AMBIVALENT. This word is sometimes misused for *ambiguous. Ambivalent,* a term from psychoanalysis, means that two irreconcilable emotions are operating in the mind (love-hate, for example). *Mixed feelings* is a less pretentious substitute. *Ambiguous* is applied only to written or spoken statements and means "having two or more possible meanings": *The employer was ambivalent about the applicant because of his ambiguous answers.*

ANTIQUE. The trouble with *antique* is that it is both a noun and an adjective. An antique is a rare old object. An antique clock is a rare old clock. If you want to describe a rare old store, you could conceivably call it an antique store. But if you mean a store that trades in rare old objects, it is an *antiques* store. A person who deals in *antique* objects is an *antiques* dealer.

ANYMORE. When the *Webster III* dictionary came out, language purists were shocked that it permitted *any more* to be written as one word, *anymore.* Well, all right (NEVER *alright*), I don't like it a lot (NEVER *alot*), but will go along—with this reservation: When you're writing about something additional, make it two words: *I don't want any more advice from you.* When it's used as an adverb, as in, *I don't want to argue with that editor anymore,* go ahead and make it one word. By the way, if you've ever written *some place* as one word, don't do it anymore.

BOTTOM LINE. Leave it to accountants and bookkeepers. When used metaphorically for outcome, result or consequence (intended or otherwise), it's just another impoverished cliché. "For Public School 27, excellence is the bottom line." It probably isn't even true.

CHARISMA. Properly a theological term for the special grace that gives saints their power; a divine gift. For lesser mortals, *appeal, magnetism* and *attractiveness* are all more appropriate. Nowadays, *charisma* is used for any politician with a smooth voice and a knack for getting votes.

CHILLING EFFECT. The lawyer who first thought this one up deserved a round of applause. But that was years ago, and since then the phrase has become as stale as three-day-old bread. Court decisions adverse to the press, for example, are said to have a chilling effect on free speech and some kinds of reporting. Get up to normal room temperature by using *inhibit, curtail* or *restrict*. It may be OK when referring to informal processes, but you probably can be more specific.

COMMUNITY. For some reason, perhaps because the bonds that make up a true community are scarce and getting scarcer, the noun is applied these days to professions, occupations and virtually any conglomeration of people sharing peripheral interests. So we see *medical community, engineering community* and *business community*, and may soon see *trash collectors' community*. Write *doctors, engineers, business (people)* and, by all means, *trash collectors*. And don't even think of *world community*. This silly term is much used by diplomats, politicians and other pomposities. Just look at the real world, with its constant wars, rebellions, national, ethnic and racial animosities—this is a "community"?

CONCEPT. Pompous noun for *idea, notion, scheme*. Use one of those less grand words unless you're referring to something complex, like Einstein's concept of the universe, or Kung's concept of the church. Not *the mayor's new concept of parking lot use*. (Be careful of *notion*, though. It's often used as a sneer word, meaning a sort of harebrained idea: *He had a notion he could halt the arms race.*)

CONCEPTUALIZE. Same thing. Fit for, say, an effort to conceptualize the movement of subatomic particles. But why bother? What's wrong with *envision*?

CONFRONTATION. An all-purpose word from the seething sixties that has long since turned mushy. When possible, reach for the specifics: *noisy argument, shoving match, scuffle, exchange of insults, ultimatum*.

CONVINCE, PERSUADE. *Convince* requires a state of mind, *persuade* a course of action. A person often acts in accordance with convictions, but not necessarily. An editor may try to convince you that a lead is poor; failing that, he may persuade you to change it anyway. The distinction is valuable and should be preserved. Think: convince *that*, persuade *to*.

DEFINING MOMENT. Mostly humbug. Just to take one former president, what was George Bush's defining moment? His election as president? His "read my lips" promise? His breaking of said promise? His victory over Iraq? His electoral defeat shortly thereafter, one defining moment undefining the other? Most lives have several defining moments, and contemporaries are ill equipped to judge them.

DICHOTOMY. "A split or division into two contradictory or mutually exclusive parts": truth and falsehood, right and wrong. *Split* or *division* is always preferable in news writing.

DILEMMA. If we restrict this word (or any word) to its precise meaning, we keep its usefulness. *Dilemma* is not a synonym of *predicament* or *jam* or *trouble*. Someone in a dilemma faces two alternative courses of action, either of which is likely to be unpleasant. "*On* the horns of a dilemma" is a cliché to be avoided, but it does illustrate the special problem the word defines.

DISINTERESTED. Does not mean *uninterested*. *Disinterested* means personally detached, unbiased in a matter in which one has no stake. *Uninterested* simply means lacking interest. You can be disinterested in your friend's divorce without being at all uninterested. As a reporter, you should always be disinterested but never uninterested.

EXCELLENCE, PURSUIT OF. Shopworn to the point anything associated with excellence should never be, this is a favored, if immodest, characterization by certain professional groups of their current scrambling. Sometimes unavoidable in direct quotes; use with extreme caution at other times.

EXIT (as a verb). Originally favored by flight attendants ("Please exit the plane by the rear doors"), it's now used by bus drivers and a lot of other people. To convert a noun into a verb is ancient practice and honorable if the recycled verb is needed. In this case, you have perfectly good words already: *leave, depart, get out.* Airline people also say *deplane.* Will we have *debus* next?

EXPECT/ANTICIPATE. Politicians and others given to pretentiousness often substitute *anticipate* for *expect*. The words do not mean the same thing and the distinction should be kept. To *expect* is simply "to look ahead to." *Citrus growers expect about the same production as last year.* The word *anticipate* means "*to* look ahead to—and do something about it." *They put smudge pots in the groves, anticipating frost.*

EXPLICATE. If you like *replicate*, you'll love *explicate*, a pompous word for *explain*. Literary critics embrace it to sound important: *Nowhere is Mr. Thomas's exegesis more clearly explicated* …. Extricate me!

FARTHER/FURTHER. Correct usage requires *farther* when speaking of literal distance; *further* in all other instances. *My desk is farther from the water cooler than yours. Your daughter is further along in school than mine.* But be careful. The expression *taking it a step further,* for example, is correct because *step* is used metaphorically, not as a literal measure of distance.

FEWER/LESS. That beer does not have *less* calories, that beer has *fewer* calories. *Less* applies to quantities, *fewer* to numbers. Ironclad rule: *Less* modifies a singular noun, *fewer* modifies a plural noun. *Fewer* calories, *less* taste.

FLAUNT/FLOUT. A TV announcer reported, "Doctors with MD plates sometimes flaunt the law." *Flaunt* means "to boastfully exhibit." If you've got it, flaunt it. *Flout* means "defy." What the doctors did with the MD plates was flout the law and flaunt their profession.

FORTUNATE/FORTUITOUS. Although some, seeking pomposity, substitute *fortuitous* for *fortunate*, the words are not synonymous. *Fortunate* means "lucky." *Fortuitous* means "by chance," "by accident." Something that is *fortuitous* can also be *fortunate*, but unless it happened by chance, *fortunate* is the correct word: *It was fortunate that the plane had enough fuel to reach an alternate landing field. The pilot's choice was fortuitous; all the other fields were damaged.*

FOUNDER/FLOUNDER. *Without steam, the pumps could not function and the ship began to flounder and go down.* No, it didn't. It began to *founder,* that is, "to collapse, to break down suddenly." To *flounder* means "to move clumsily, awkwardly, in confusion"—probably a blend of *founder* and *blunder.* (When that foundering ship sank, a flounder [noun] might have watched.)

FROM … TO. This construction denotes a logical progression, as from A to Z, or from girlhood to womanhood, or from stockroom to boardroom, or from soup to nuts. To write *activities that range from golf to investing* begs the question; what goes between? To write *from golf to investing to racing to poker* is worse. What you probably mean is, *as diverse as.* If so, say so.

FULSOME. It does not mean "lavish" or "bountiful," as in *fulsome praise.* It means "revolting, noisome." The word is now so often misused that a lot of people will misunderstand when you use it correctly. The literate, who are also part of the readership, will applaud. This does, however, raise the point of *fulsome*'s usefulness. There are plenty of substitutes.

HOPEFUL/FEARFUL. *They were fearful that he might be ill, and hopeful that he would recover.* A $10,000 reward for proof that these words improve upon, *They were grateful that he had returned, feared he might be ill and hoped he would recover.* (The battle against *hopefully,* used in the sense of *"we hope"* [*Hopefully, the Dodgers will win the pennant.*] seems hopeless— but fight on.) These formulations have already betrayed at least one writer into *she said shamefully,* when she meant *shamefacedly.* For shame.

ICON. Originally the painted or sculpted image of a saint or other religious figure, which then became an object of veneration in its own right. Now-adays, *icon,* unless used in a computer-related context, is a wilted cliché, applied to the famous and third- or second-raters in any field of endeavor. A good word to avoid.

IMPACT (as a verb). Technically, impact can be used as verb without run-ning afoul of grammatical standards. But it's an ineffective verb that merely tells us something had an effect, without characterizing the effect. Maybe we can get it from context, but *Newspaper editors listened to a presentation on how new technology would impact the industry* doesn't give us much insight.

INFER/IMPLY. *The official complained that the newspaper story falsely inferred that he had condoned racial hatred.* The word the writer intended was implied. *Infer* means "to deduce or judge from evidence." *Imply* means "to intimate, to signify, to hint."

INNOVATIVE. Ridden hard by advertising copywriters and institutional and political boasters and propagandists, this adjective is nearly exhausted. Few programs, policies or people are truly original. Reserve the word for such rare instances. Renaming three courses in its curriculum doesn't make Podunk College an *innovative* school.

INPUT. Nice computer term, so let's keep it in the technical kennel. In human affairs, warm-blooded words are better: *They sought a stronger voice,* or *a greater say, at city hall,* not *more input.*

INTERFACE. A technical word from science and engineering that jar-goneers find irresistible. It means a connection between independent systems, as between a computer and a typesetting machine. Showoffs apply it to human relations, where *coordination, agreement, something in common* and *shared* are all better terms. They also use it as a verb. *Doctors and nurses should interface more in a hospital setting* might be tough if many wear glasses. Why not work together? Do we interface on this point?

JURIST. Not just a substitute or synonym for plain "judge" or "lawyer." A jurist is someone deeply learned in the law, a legal scholar. Some judges may be jurists, but the run-of-the-mill judge is about as deeply learned in the law as your average ambulance chaser.

KUDOS. The Greeks had a word for it, and it was *kydos*, meaning "glory." It has come to us almost intact as *kudos*, meaning "acclaim in recognition of achievement." It is a good word to avoid because it often sounds wrong when used correctly, as in *kudos is in order for Joe Smith*. It is a singular noun in the same way that *pathos*, of similar Greek origin, is singular. There is no such word as *kudo*, just as there is no such word as *patho*. If you simply avoid *kudos*, it will be to your glory.

LEGEND, LEGENDARY. Need no longer be confined to mythical heroes (Hercules) but can be extended to living people (Streisand, Tom Cruise), moderns (DiMaggio) and famous historical figures. Be careful, though. The words are clichés, on the same low level as *icon*. Find something better, or omit; usually, the name suffices.

LIFESTYLE. Overworked vogue word, usually just a glossy way of saying "life" or "way of living." *After years of comfort and luxury, financial setbacks changed his lifestyle* (life). *Some Acapulcans have a splendid lifestyle* (live splendidly). It is time for this trendy locution to die, in style.

LITERALLY. Disastrous as a casual intensifier because it means that something is factually and precisely true. *The Mets literally slaughtered the Cardinals last night* would have left at least nine corpses. I would never use *literally* in a million years. I mean that figuratively.

MEDIA. This word is plural. The press is a news medium; television is a medium; radio is a medium. Together, they are news media. Never write, *The media is sometimes guilty of bad grammar*. Write, *The media <u>are</u> ...*

MILITATE/MITIGATE. The words are confusing because they sound and look alike. They aren't in the least similar in meaning. *Militate* (from the Latin word for "soldier") means "to have weight or effect." *Mitigate* (from the Latin "to soften") means just that: "to soften, make less severe or painful, alleviate, mollify." *The judge <u>mitigated</u> the sentence from 30 days to 10.*

The unpredictable economy militates against long-term planning. Choose plainer words.

MOTHER NATURE. Often so invoked, playfully or otherwise. Nature may seem maternal when benign, but also sends floods, earthquakes, hurricanes, tornadoes, and the like. And in animal life, nature—as Tennyson described her more realistically—is "red in tooth and claw," not exactly maternal.

NAVAL. This maritime adjective sometimes comes out navel, always good for a belly laugh. The variety of orange, though, is correctly navel, because that's what that scar resembles where it was attached, umbilically, to a blossom.

NOTION. See CONCEPT.

NOUNS INTO VERBS. Turning nouns into verbs is a long and honorable tradition: *to telephone, to cable,* and, more recently, *to text. To contact* is borderline usage, handy only when the nature of the contact is nebulous: letter, telephone call, native runner? But draw the line at noun-spawned verbs that serve no real need and sound gushy, like *debut, host* and *author.* People *make their debuts, give parties* and *write books.* Especially execrable is *debut* in the past tense: *The new edition debuted three months ago.*

OBJECTIVE. No one important likes to have a mere aim or goal, but an objective. In most uses, *aim* or *goal* is better.

ONLY. Be careful where you place this trouble-fraught little modifier. Put *only* before any word in the following seven-word sentence and you get seven different meanings: *I hit him in the eye yesterday.* But don't get pedantic about it. In such commonly understood phrases as I only want orange juice, placement of *only* where it strictly belongs (before *orange juice*) seems stilted. I'm only trying to help.

OPTION. If you don't like this word, which bureaucrats and academic babblers have made *de rigueur,* you have an option: *choice.* Same with the verb *opt*: choose *choose.*

PERCEIVE. Blown-up word for *see, understand, grasp* or *realize,* spewn into the conversational mainstream via academia. Through overuse for the sake of perceptual elegance, it is also becoming a weasel word, beclouding the obvious. *Jamaica's economic decline under Prime Minister Manley was perceived as a major cause of his defeat.* Perceived, because it was. Omit *perceived as.*

PLUS. Advertisers kidnapped this innocent word from mathematicians as a trendy replacement for *also,* or *moreover* or *not only that,* none of which needs replacing. Let us restore *plus* to the mathematicians. Minus, never start a sentence with it.

PRAGMATIC. Imported from philosophy, where it describes the intellectual acceptance of whatever is workable as "true," or at least sound. A pragmatist may dislike phonics in principle, but accept it as a workable way to teach reading. But if somebody knows how to deal with insurance salesmen, bank statements and a leaky faucet, he's not pragmatic, he's practical.

PRE-DAWN DARKNESS. Hackneyed journalese. Write *pre-dawn darkness* if you're also prepared to write *pre-dusk brightness*. It is a poetic phrase that has been worked to death, that's all. A substitute is needed. How about *ere Aurora arose*? No? Then let us return, simply, to *before dawn*.

PRESTIGIOUS. This, along with *coveted*, is an automatic modifier that pops up drearily with *award, trophy* and *honor*. You even see the *prestigious Nobel Prize* and the *coveted Pulitzer Prize*. It goes without saying, so don't say it.

REASON WHY. When *reason* is used as a noun, try never to follow it with *why*. The reason I urge this (not the *reason why* I urge this) is to reduce clutter. *Why* after *reason* is almost always superfluous. When the tone is conversational, though, it's sometimes hard to avoid the *why*—but I see no reason why rules should not have exceptions, do you?

REFER. *Refer back* is a tautology; it's the only way to go. Same is true of *revert back*. That *re-* prefix means "back." Redundant. However, *referred* is much better than *referenced*, which is among the most superfluous noun-to-verb additions to the language.

REFUTE/REBUT. A subtle distinction here, but important, especially in journalism, to avoid editorializing unwittingly. *Refute* renders a verdict; it means "to disprove, to demolish an argument." *Rebut* means "to answer charges or allegations by counter-argument." Even though most dictionaries give *rebut* the secondary meaning of "disprove," the word isn't safe. *Reply to, contend* and *contradict* are neutral substitutes for *rebut* and probably better than *refute*.

RELATE TO. A vogue term, probably from the social sciences, with a dogged power of endurance. Its vagueness masks any interesting specifics of the relationship. If little Mary fails to relate to her peers, she may be a bully, she may be shy, or she may limp. For these or other reasons, she can't seem to make friends. That's a human way of putting it.

REMAINS TO BE SEEN. A favorite phrase in punditry and some news analyses. Because everything in the future remains to be seen, this line (often the last in a story) is as weak as a newborn fawn and not nearly as graceful. An equally self-evident variant: "Only time will tell."

REPLICATE. Scientists like to use *replicate* instead of *repeat exactly*, or *duplicate*. Let 'em.

SCENARIO. Tom Barber, word-watcher at the *Milwaukee Journal*, calls it "one of those tiresome Watergate words, coined by a bunch of generals, probably, as they plotted deploying their deterrent firepower to neutralize an aggressor." Amen. Barber made a list of 99 alternate words. He wasn't even breathing hard.

SELF-CONFESSED. Until you discover a way for someone to confess in another person's behalf, write *confessed*.

SKILLS. Pedagogues' padding. *Mastering mathematical skills, teaching reading skills.* Make it *mastering mathematics, teaching to read.*

SOPHISTICATED. A clichéd adjective that writers apply to any piece of technology that's over their heads. Computers, as a class, for example, are no longer so remarkable that they need to be tagged as sophisticated. Neither are F-16s. Because so much is, in comparison with the ordinary writer's mechanical aptitude, sophisticated, the adjective should be used sparingly.

SPELLING. The English language embraces so many variations in spelling that some words, like the multiplication tables, just have to be memorized. Start with these 20 and add your own: *accommodate, affidavit, asinine, consensus, diphtheria, embarrass, harass, imposter, impresario, inoculate, liquefy, pavilion, precede, rarefy, resuscitate, rococo, sacrilegious, siege, supersede, titillate.*

STANCE. Means primarily a standing position, as a fighter or golfer might take. Now it is used for *attitude, position, philosophy: his foreign policy stance.* There's nothing drastically wrong with it except that it's becoming worn out, like *posture.*

STRATEGY. Bowwow language. Use *plan, scheme, design* or *method. The housing agency has several strategies for dealing with urban poverty* sounds important in a handout, which is why it's there. Make it *has several ways of dealing with poverty.* Academics, of course, talk about *new strategies in curricular reform,* but there is no reforming them.

SUBSUME. As soon as academics began sprinkling their learned papers with this vogue word, bureaucrats jumped all over it. Most of them misuse it. *Subsume* means "to include within a larger group." *The question of twice-weekly garbage pickup was subsumed by the debate over the whole municipal budget.* Probably because it looks and sounds like consume, some mistakenly take it to mean "to eat up." Don't you.

SUPPORTIVE OF. Why weaken a decent verb by turning it into an adjective with a preposition? *He was supportive of the fund drive?* What mush. *He supported the fund drive.*

SURROGATE. Hard to know, or judge, how this word invaded political babble, as in *the president's surrogates. Representatives, stand-ins* and *substitutes* are better words, although politicians will prefer the more imposing one.

TENSIONS, RELAXATION OF. A staple of diplomatic language, where vagueness is often useful. Overblown when used for more mundane affairs, such as a school board squabbling with teachers or a baseball manager at odds with the owner. (Is it a *détente* if they become friendly again?) *The fact that contract negotiations with the meat packers resumed signaled a relaxation of tensions.* Make it *brightened hopes for a settlement,* or some such.

THRUST. Doesn't blast off quite as frequently as it used to, but it's still tired and, by association with the types who keep using it as a noun, pompous. *The thrust of the 21-page report ....* Make it *gist, tenor, drift* or *burden.*

UTILIZE. There is no discernible reason why anyone would want to substitute that verb for *use.* They have exactly the same meaning, so why choose the longer and uglier word over the short and crisp one? Use *use.*

VERBAL/ORAL. *Verbal* applies to any use of language, either spoken or written. *Oral* applies to spoken language only. *He made a verbal commitment* is nonsense.

VIABLE. In its original sense in the life sciences, *viable* means "capable of survival and growth." Now it is used for *real, workable, practical, sound* or *healthy.* If those splendid words needed technical reinforcement, *viable* would be all right. But there is no need for it, and, besides, misuse robs *viable* of a limited and precise meaning.

VIABLE ALTERNATIVE. Used in *viable*'s (regrettably) expanded sense to mean "a sound or workable alternative." But does anyone ever seek an unsound or unworkable alternative? The adjective is redundant; leave it out. The same often applies to modifiers for *solution* and *option.*

VIRTUAL. It doesn't mean "actual," and it doesn't mean "nearly," either. *Virtual* describes something that has the effect but not the form. *When the president resigned, the vice president became the virtual head of the company* (even though he had not been so named).

WHENCE, ALBEIT, WHEREIN, THUS. All somewhat archaic and therefore (not *hence*) undesirable. But if you must use *whence*, it means "from where"; *from whence* is a tautology.

WORKAHOLIC. This was bright coinage back when it identified a person truly addicted to work. Now it has been reduced to describing anyone who stays late at the office. Time to put it aside to dry out—along with all the other *-aholics*: *cleanaholic* (tidy housekeeper), *runaholic* (jogger) and, so help me, *wordaholic* (scrupulous editor). I need a drink.

YOUTH. A respectable noun that few ever use in conversation. You talk about *children, adolescents, teenagers, young people, the youth of America,* perhaps, but can you hear yourself saying, *Suzie next door is an interesting youth?* No? Then think twice before you use the word in copy.

---

* The (Toronto) *Globe and Mail* quoted a doctor who carried the locution to the absurd: "If someone is confronted with certain knowledge that he or she is going to die a painful death through terminal illness, then suicide can be a viable option."

News Writing for the Digital Age— an Introduction

If you are reading this book, you are probably well aware that the media world is in significant tumult due to shifts driven by new technologies. For most of the 20th century, newspapers and television mediated between message senders and their audiences. To get information to the public, message senders needed either to attract the interest of a reporter or buy an advertisement in a media product. Today, those message senders have their own websites and social media channels to reach the public, meaning the financial footing of traditional media industries has softened. Replacing that revenue will be the industry's top challenge for the foreseeable future—one that may force journalists to rethink what the profession looks like.

What you've read so far is a timeless approach to the fundamentals of journalistic writing. Writing clear declarative sentences will never go out of style. As the sociologist Robert Park wrote in 1940, the purpose of news is to orient us in the world. If news stories confuse, they estrange a reader from his or her society. The goal of journalism is to make things more clear, and that starts at the sentence level.

The purpose of journalism is to deliver information to readers that enhances their ability to participate in civic life. This can take the form of helping readers understand issues being argued in front of government bodies, or learning about cultural events in the community, or even finding out high school football scores. Journalism *produces* news.

The important thing about this view of journalism is that it is not tied to any specific platform. Digital journalism uses a range of technologies to produce news and relies on the internet to disseminate that news. From a production perspective, this has expanded the ways we can tell stories. The written word is still many people's favorite format, but now we have video, audio, and even data visualization to complement text or even replace it entirely.

Yet, the message is still news, regardless of how it is disseminated, and the news is created by journalists—even when the written word is minimal or replaced by something else. The need to inform and explain has not changed. The tips included here are not simply aesthetic; they speak to the effectiveness of the journalistic message.

There are advantages to these new developments in the media world. A digital journalist is not restricted by the limitations of print, and can now match the story to the most effective storytelling medium. In addition, the modern journalist can interact in something like real time with audiences, sharing details and answering questions to help make the stories land more effectively.

Of course, there are downsides to internet journalism; speed often leads to mistakes, and even accurate stories may be topped with salacious headlines that end up overshadowing good work. To be successful in journalism today, each reporter must learn to navigate the new journalistic landscape in addition to mastering the fundamental newswriting skills covered in the earlier chapters of this book. The formats and storytelling styles may change, but the future of journalism will be built atop content that is focused on helping readers make their way in the world.

Chapter 14

The New Media: Writing for the Web

To the dismay of journalists and their bosses, the days of people curling up with a print newspaper are dwindling. Decreased circulation and falling advertising revenues mean that traditional newspapers are finding new ways to survive in a changing landscape, reshaping the context in which journalists operate. Today, most of us get our news through online sources, be they the websites of legacy news organizations or digital-only publications.

Most of the old rules still apply. Clarity still matters, as does accuracy. One major difference with online writing is that writers no longer deal with a limited physical space for their stories. While it is tempting to flaunt your eloquence in the expanded format, remember that readers still have limited attention spans. The goal of newswriting is to share stories and information for the benefit of your readers, not to have your self-indulgent prose sit mostly unread in a long-forgotten browser tab.

Strong leads and attributions still matter for the same reasons. News organizations chart scroll depth on stories, so they can tell when readers fall away paragraph by paragraph. "Get the information into the top of the story" is an old journalistic lesson. In the classic film *His Girl Friday*, editor Walter Burns responds to a story by reporter Hildy Johnson by asking, "Who's going to read the second paragraph?" Today, he would ask, "Who's going to scroll that far?" They are the same question.

From a storytelling perspective, the digital transition gives us a larger toolbox with which to tell our stories. We are no longer limited to the written word, as web-based news allows us to integrate audio and video.

Reporters can make use of social media, allowing them to communicate more directly with their readers and even collect information from them. In addition, the internet excels at collecting metrics, so it is now possible for a writer to know exactly what interests his or her audience the most, end even to direct ("push") items to a particular audience based on their interests. We will talk about some of these new tools in the next chapter. For now, it is important to know that web platforms allow us to amass many different media formats in the same place.

The best example of this might be the news "liveblogs" that news organizations like *The Guardian* and *The New York Times* use for breaking events. Each entry is a lead of its own, a distillation of the data points being added to the coverage as the story develops. In those unfolding reports, they bring together reporting, newsmaker tweets, video, photos and other graphic elements in the same place to address multiple aspects of an unfolding story.

The newswriting process still starts with trying to figure out the best lead. But the next question is, are words the best and only way to tell this story?

HEADLINES

For the reader, the experience of consuming news online is much different from reading a traditional newspaper. Research shows that people absorb less of an article's meaning when read online as compared to reading from a paper. As news writers, it is important that we accommodate this tendency. Every journalist wants his or her material to be read, and—more importantly—every news service needs readers in order to stay in business.

Today, search traffic and social media referrals are the ways readers find stories, and for that reason, headlines have become the new news leads. The headline has become more important than ever in the digital age.

How to be Found

Modern news writers need to take steps to make their work more discoverable for potential readers. With the advent of internet searching engines came the development of "key words" and searchable terms. Search engines such as Google or Bing work by using "web crawlers" to index content. Once the web crawlers have determined the nature of a story, they can deliver it to internet users who ask for it by searching for specific words or terms. However, many times the internet already "knows" a reader's interests based on information it has collected over a period of time, and, as such, it may deliver the article to that individual, unasked, via a news service.

Some of the most popular news sites don't produce news at all, serving instead as "news aggregators." Google News and Apple News, for instance, merely aggregate news from other sources and deliver it to users based on their interests. Usually, users can define their own areas of interest, but sites can also track the items a user has clicked on and feed him or her stories that are similar in nature. It is important that a writer select appropriate words identifying the article in order to reach the maximum number of readers.

Using keywords and heavily searched terms helps make stories more discoverable, whether in the headline or in the body of the article. If you are writing about a well-known political figure's new policy proposal, headlines should include the name of the politician and searchable terms related to the proposal. If you are writing about a soccer player, mention his or her team. This will help readers find your story.

Enhancing your story for searchability should not be done at the price of clarity or truth. The good news for news writers is that strong writing tends to align with what the search engines want.

In digital media, headlines tend to be longer because they must be able to stand on their own. Articles in traditional newspapers bolster the effect of their headlines by placing photos or subheaders in the proximity of the article. This works less well in digital spaces because readers do not have other related information within their view as they scroll through Twitter.

Search engines are programmed to distinguish quality content from nonsense; they use algorithms that look for markers of quality. One clue is thematic coherence within a story. News stories have an advantage here because they are usually about a single topic which is named in the headline and referred to throughout the story. Well-structured stories are a sign of strong writing. Using subheaders is one way to signal that to the search engines.

One of the other clues search engines use to rank articles are clicks and shares. As such, if your story is well-liked, it stands a better chance of catching the attention of other internet users. Building a relationship with your audience can be helpful in this regard, as even a small group of readers can produce the volume of clicks and shares that may elevate your story's ranking in a search engine.

Clickbait

Writing to integrate searchable terms may feel uncomfortable for some journalists, but using headlines to draw in readers is well within the boundaries of journalistic ethics. The important thing is to ensure your headline does not degrade into *clickbait*—a headline that distorts or exaggerates stories to earn page views. Its purpose is not to inform, but to take advantage of readers' curiosity so that they will click, thus raising the number of views the site can claim. For example, the 2015 *New York Post* headline "Johnny Manziel receiver admits to randomly killing jogger," had nothing to do with the quarterback. Rather, a former college teammate had confessed to a crime. The headline used the name of a more famous teammate—someone more likely to have his name typed into Google—to attract search traffic. Manziel had no other connection to this story. News should inform, not distort.

STRUCTURING STORIES

Beginning journalism students learn structures like the "inverted pyramid" or "kebob" to manage the basic flow of news writing. The inverted pyramid—the standard approach to a straight news story—ranks information from most important to least, with the key takeaway in the lead. The kebob structure is more common in feature writing, with attention-grabbing anecdotes or quotes at the top and bottom of each story and exposition in the middle.

These formats have migrated from analog to digital journalism, but writing for the screen instead of the page creates new demands. Writing longer stories that incorporate multimedia elements requires a structure than can accommodate them. That means more pressure on the writer to maintain momentum in a story.

Subheaders, or subheads, are common in print writing, but they are essential in digital formats. Long reads can be daunting, and signposts make it easier for audiences to figure out how information fits together. You can think of a trail of subheads as analogous to an outline, helping the reader to understand how the information is sequenced while also indicating of the key point of each section. Keep in mind that you know where your story is going, but the reader is usually encountering the information for the first time. The longer the story, the easier it is to get lost. Any story longer than 500 words may be helped by breaking it up into sections.

Subheads should be descriptive, often quotations or mini-headlines within a story to help maintain reader interest in a longer piece. Bringing in other storytelling elements—like pictures or videos—also creates orderly structures for a story. A structure that is easy to follow promotes clarity, which helps readers make sense of their world.

LINKING

Sourcing and quoting are ways journalists buttress their authority. We are experts on news writing, so we ask other people for their analyses of the economy or yesterday's football game. Today, most newspapers use a complex content management system (CMS) to administer digital content and promote collaboration. Access to information within the CMS offers web-based news writers the opportunity to **hyperlink** to an article from the past or to information published elsewhere. Hyperlinking can save words and also makes text on a screen easier for the eye to follow. Most CMSs embed links in a different color with underlines. The colored underlines acts as a differentiator, signposts to direct readers to interesting information on a screen.

Insert hyperlinks atop descriptive text to maintain the flow in your writing. A construction like this doesn't work:

> Congress posted the report over the attorney general's protestations. The report can be found here.

The reader is presented with an empty sentence that introduces no new information. Observe this more effective presentation, which uses descriptive link text (i.e., the link is a relevant part of the sentence):

> Congress posted the report over the attorney general's protestations.

If you are writing for a smaller web outlet, links also create connections between websites. Most online sites can see where traffic comes from, which may create connections and synergies between sites, enhancing your own visibility. Also, search engines like descriptive link text.

It is important, of course, to link with care. Think of it as being similar to quoting. Inserting a hyperlink into your story means vouching for the quality of the site to which you are linking. Linking to a flawed published report raises questions about your own reporting, as does misrepresenting what the linked page says.

SOCIAL SHARING AS A JOURNALIST

As stated earlier, journalism is changing. We now have a collection of what Harvard Law School professor Yochai Benkler calls "the new, networked media." In addition to traditional journalism outlets, news writers must now produce material for websites, blogs, social media, YouTube and more.

Dr. Benkler does not necessarily view the emergence of new media as problematic, though it's definitely a shift that is disrupting both viewing habits and the business models of existing media purveyors. He believes that traditional media and the "new, networked media" have come together in a new media environment.

Today, sharing on social media is how news finds its audience, and vice versa. There is no secret to getting a story to go viral; what matters most is interest—either in the person tweeting or in the subject matter. However, since news or opinions can now be published by anybody with a computer (or even a smartphone), it is important that each writer make the most of his or her professional skills to produce superior content that will stand out.

One of the best ways to make people take notice of a tweet or a story is to include images in the post. In general, emphasis on broadcast or other multimedia elements will help your click-through rate—the ratio of how many users view a page versus how many click on a specific link within that page. We will discuss multimedia elements further in the next chapter.

Social media also offers an opportunity for reporters to build reputations—something increasingly important as more writers turn to freelance work, without the inherent credibility of a news reporting organization to back them up. Journalists in this situation often take on a curation role, sharing information relevant to their subject area from their own stories as well as other outlets. Political reporters cannot be everywhere, but a good Twitter follow links to relevant stories he or she did not write.

Posting to social media allows writers to form new sorts of relationships with their audiences. If done effectively, this approach can create a built-in audience for your work. While there are a myriad of social networking platforms among which to choose, two of the most important are blogging and Twitter.

Blogs and Blogging

In today's news environment, it is advisable that every reporter—especially free-lance reporters—maintain a blog (from the words "web" and "log"). Blogs allowing the writer to nurture a community of readers who appreciate his or her writing either because of subject matter or, in some cases, the "voice" of the writer. In a small way, the reporter becomes an online personality.

The rules for blogs are different than those of traditional print and broadcasting. The chief differences are in tone, frequency and structure. A blog is somewhat like a conversation between the writer and reader. As such, the tone is typically less formal than traditional news writing. Speed and frequency of posting are the highest priorities here.

Blog entries do not typically tell the entire story. Since blogs are designed to be tight and quick, the writer can initiate the blog story with a quick fact as soon as it is known, even if much of the information is not yet available. In fact, the mere expectation of news is a valid blog entry. As the story continues to develop, the writer may provide an update at each step. The result is a series of posts displayed in reverse chronological order. If you present your blog entries timely and accurately, you may develop a reputation as the best source of information on a particular topic.

Twitter

Twitter is a combination of blogging, texting and instant messaging; it has also been referred to as a "microblog." The platform enables "microbloggers" to send a constant stream of updates right from their laptops and smartphones.

Twitter restricts the size of each message (tweet) to a maximum of 280 characters. By capping the size of tweets, Twitter forces each entry to be short and, if done well, succinct. It also makes tweets easy to review; a reader can scan entries from hundreds of users at a glance. All of these features combine to make Twitter a popular social media platform.

Because it is so pervasive and user-friendly, it is no surprise to find a great deal of rubbish on Twitter. However, the number of Twitter users who produce useful content is growing. These users include professional journalists as well as amateurs, some of whom contribute new information, and some who share content from other sources.

The Speed of News

Time is of the essence in online reporting. Some stories move so fast and are reported online so quickly that they don't even make it into a traditional newspaper. An accident on the interstate, for example, may be over and done within a matter of hours. During this time, an online reporter may report the traffic delay and provide multiple updates, whereas a newspaper—if it covers the incident at all—will be reporting the story the next day completely in past tense.

The rise of the new media does bring up several questions related to the practice of journalism. For instance, can a blogger be considered a journalist, based solely on his or her blog? In the view of most journalism-related codes of ethics, not usually. The argument is that journalists deal in facts, which they acquire through research and interviews with subject-matter experts and eyewitnesses. Bloggers tend to deal mostly with opinions and analysis. (To be fair, many of these opinions and analyses are thoughtful, articulate and well-reasoned.) Rather than "journalist," the term being used—sometimes derisively—to describe bloggers, vloggers (video blog) and web-based pundits is "media influencer."

Many of the "news" bloggers and websites lack a commitment to objectivity and professionalism; this affects their credibility, of course, though it doesn't seem to affect their appeal. (Of course, it may be that the same could be said about some traditional news outlets.) Some new media outlets, though, have begun to acquire reputations for objectivity and accuracy, often in niche areas; some cybersecurity blogs, for instance, are trusted primary sources of information in that area. It's possible that we will end up with a solid collection of new media outlets that we've learned to trust—and which have earned that trust.

Most importantly, a journalistic voice on social media should be committed to providing true and accurate information; it is very important to check the source of tweets and confirm posts before sharing. Any tweet or post may be taken out of context or used to accuse the writer of bias. Be cautious when selecting the sources you use, and think of them as endorsements. Ironically, in this age of misinformation, your reputation as an accurate and reliable journalist is more valuable than ever.

Chapter 15

Writing Beyond Reading— Broadcast Journalism

When the first edition of this book was published in 1982, the internet was used mainly by a few scientists at a couple of universities. Now, of course, the internet has a constant presence in most of our lives and, for our purposes, is a common conduit for news. For those in journalism, the emergence of the web required a re-evaluation of how news is shared with the public. Today when you check news websites, you might see its broadcast stories recast for print formats. Most newspaper websites host video and audio content now, something they could not do before. Your local TV stations very likely produce online versions of the stories on the evening news for their website. Today, when we speak of broadcast journalism, we cannot omit web-based broadcasting.

Along with the mix of traditional journalism outlets, we've recently added websites, blogs, social media, YouTube, and more to the list of sources we scour for news stories. Millennials, especially, get much of their news from social networking sites such as Facebook and Twitter. Only some 24% of millennials still watch television for news, and about 38% of all adults get most or all of their news online. Digital media wields much of the power that used to belong to traditional media.

It is easy for those who view themselves as defenders of the written word to be intimidated by these formats, overwhelmed by the technology it takes to produce multimedia stories or dismissive of media that they perceive to be inadequate to capture the complexity of the world. But those concerns should take a back seat to the work of journalism. The job is to inform your audience, and that includes reaching the audience wherever it is.

This chapter lays out some of the general principles of writing for broadcast formats. Television news, radio news, and web-based news have their own distinct quirks, conventions, and approaches. The basic goal of conveying the news accurately and clearly, however, has not changed.

WRITING FOR THE EAR

This guide includes many pages decrying the ways writers overload sentences, which tends to obscure more than it illuminates. In print, a committed reader could theoretically go back over a sloppy sentence to decipher it (they don't, but they could). A person driving a car cannot go backward to take a second shot at a complex sentence. Neither will the person listening to an online video while working in another tab or running the news in the background while they chop onions for dinner. Those people simply disregard whatever information they do not catch. Or worse, they end up confused, emerging with an incorrect understanding of the story's message.

The ear discerns less than the eye. Readers can sometimes visually navigate a clogged print paragraph that—if spoken aloud—would be completely unintelligible. The advantage of most broadcast formats is that the words do not have to do all the work by themselves. Multimedia reporters use images and sounds to buttress their words. In the hands of a skilled news writer, the pictures and words complement each other to create a more effective story. The trick is to determine when the picture really is worth a thousand words or if you, as the writer, need to chip in a couple of syllables to balance the transaction.

THE CORE ELEMENTS

Chapter 3 discussed the importance of print leads in news writing. If a writer cannot distill the purpose of a story into a single short sentence, what hope does the reader have of understanding it? In broadcast formats, that clarity is more urgent because we need to connect disparate elements to produce a clear package. In his book, *Aim for the Heart: Write, Shoot, Report and Produce for TV and Multimedia*, journalism instructor Al Tompkins promotes a technique used by Pulitzer prize-winning writer Jon Franklin to create a focus statement for a story. Tompkins encourages writers to find the three-word description of their news package. The story's lead will be longer, but this organizing principle helps us cut away the noise.

News is not prestige television; we are trying to communicate as directly as possible. In writing for broadcast, you are mixing together three core elements to tell stories.

1. **Voiceover:** The words of the reporter or narrator telling the story

2. **Sound on Tape (SOT):** Recorded interview clips spliced into the story

3. **Natural sound:** Ambient noise related to your story, such as the sound of a marching band and fans cheering at a football game

These elements hold true whether the story has images or not. The goal is to fit them together in a way that tells a coherent story. When writing for video or creating audio slide shows, the image track adds another layer of complexity. But when you are writing for the ear, you are mixing these three audio elements in ways that make sense—which may include dropping some of the elements entirely. Many radio news reports are entirely voice-over. Some news video ignores voiceover entirely, either letting the sources narrate using SOT or using on-screen text and graphics to do that work. All choices and combinations can work, so long as the story makes sense.

WRITING A BROADCAST LEAD

In printed news, we favor the past tense. This makes sense because there is a necessary delay between an event occurring and the writing of a sentence about that event. Even the fastest typist cannot catch up with reality. (Note, though, that feature writers may try to use the present tense to place us in a scene, and they have a special license for that.)

When you have pictures or sound, however, the rules are different. Even when speaking over recorded footage, the use of multimedia places us in a location at a specific time. We are talking about what the audience is experiencing *right now*, so we speak in the present tense or present perfect tense.

Take, for example, this story about changes to rules about school nutrition. This is a reasonably straightforward print lead that makes use of the difficult question format.

> NEW YORK — Is white bread about to make a comeback on school lunch menus? After complaints about taste and costs, the Trump administration rolled back a rule that required foods like pasta and bread be made with whole grains. The cafeteria directors who lobbied for the change say they just want greater flexibility to serve foods like white bread—which are more processed and have less fiber—when whole grains don't work.

The Associated Press video package that accompanied the story used this present tense approach for the lead.

> VO: "Kids and families who rely on subsidized school lunches may be seeing some changes in their menus."

Both work for their given formats.

The print story uses words to explain what might be changing and the various political positions taken by individuals in the story. The video story opens with images of children eating school lunches in a cafeteria. A voiceover that focused on the federal government or school bureaucrats would not match the pictures. If we are being shown images of children eating, the lead should focus on that.

Radio writing is closer to writing for print, because the writer/narrator must explain the scene to the listener. Consider this lead from an NPR feature story on violence in Brazil.

> "At the dilapidated morgue in the northern Brazilian city of Natal, Director Marcos Brandao walks over the blood-smeared floor to where the corpses are kept."

The soundtrack that ran beneath that lead has the voice of the morgue's director. We can hear drawers open as well, while reporter Lulu Garcia-Navarro narrates the scene.

Writing for electronic formats does not change most of the basic rules of media writing we have already covered. We should continue to write in the active voice. Passive voice is especially bad in broadcast writing because, if we take advantage of multimedia options (which we should), we can see and hear the subjects acting. If the voiceover is passive, the images and sounds make less sense. Our explanation needs to compliment the other sensory details we are providing to our audience.

The emphasis on clean and streamlined writing is vital, because every word is an opportunity for the audience's mind to wander. Lean toward short sentences, but vary the length. Radio writing is meant to be spoken, and speech has a cadence that also conveys meaning. Long sentences are difficult for the listener to follow, and can leave the voiceover artist or newsreader gasping for breath. But a repetitive structure of nine-word sentences stacked atop each other becomes difficult to listen to. Not every sentence should have the same emphasis.

SOURCING AND ATTRIBUTING

Broadcast and multimedia journalism, like print journalism, relies heavily on quotations and analysis from experts and participants to vouch for information. But unlike print stories, broadcast scripts attribute *before* a quote or paraphrase rather than afterward.

> "The suspect's lawyer says the charges are excessive."
> "The coach says his team will be ready for tomorrow's game."

In print the attribution would come afterward.

Note also that these attributions are paraphrases. Just as when you quote in print, paraphrasing helps with clarity.

The news-reading (or listening, or watching) audience wants to hear from the participants in a story. We need to balance that, however, with our need to tell a straightforward, quick story. Most people do not speak in polished soundbites, and letting a source filibuster until he figures out what he's trying to say can take over the story. In stories about conflict, such meandering often makes the speaker sound uncertain or uninformed, and sharing the recording can create the appearance of bias. A reporter has the advantage of taking a moment or two to compose his or her thoughts and paraphrase the statement in a manner that often tells a clearer and fairer story.

In traditional commercial broadcast news, interview bites tend to last five to seven seconds. You may see longer bites than that in noncommercial sources like NPR, but even there, quotes last only 10 to 12 seconds. Interview audio may be used more extensively if you are doing documentary-style news video, but even in those cases, letting people ramble will confuse viewers. Find the sound bites that work, and construct your package around them.

SIGHT OR CITE?

One advantage of the written word over audio broadcast is that the words on the page or screen are visible, enabling readers to decode the message. We do not have that benefit in an audio broadcast context, yet knowing whether a cyclist "went fourth" or "went forth" changes the meaning of the sentence—and perhaps the entire story. When choosing words to use in a voiceover, be aware that a person listening may hear something different than was intended, even if you think it might be fully clear from the context.

Some confusing word pairs include:

- advice/advise

- affect/effect

- sight/cite

- incite/insight

- minor/miner

When easily confused words pop up in a voiceover, make sure they are as clear as possible. As the writer, you need to pay particular attention to spelling for audio broadcasting, as you do for print. Misspellings on a voiceover script can result in stumbles or mispronunciations on the air.

REMEMBER YOUR BASICS

Strong broadcast packages start with good writing. Technological sophistication cannot save an aimless broadcast package, just as complex sentences cannot dress up bad reporting. The goal of news writing is not to show how talented you are—it is to communicate accurately and clearly to your readership. Despite all the recent changes in how journalism is produced and consumed, the entire enterprise is still built on a foundation of clear sentences. Go forward with the determination to speak plainly and directly, so that your audience can better understand their world.

Notes

Notes

Notes